Introducti

The Isle of Anglesey – Ynys Môn, is ren scenery and maritime history. Most of designated Area of Outstanding Natural Beaut third of Anglesey – the largest in Wales – and Anglesey's highest point. In addition North Anglesey, Holyhead Mountain and Aberfraw Bay carry Heritage Coast status. Passing through the AONB is the 125 mile/200 km waymarked Anglesey Coastal Path, now part of the Wales Coast Path.

The AONB includes cliffs, rocky headlands and coves, award-winning sandy beaches, sand dunes, small harbours, salt marshes, woodland, heathland and a hinterland containing several low hills offering panoramic views. This diverse landscape provides a rich habitat for wildlife, including cliff nesting sites for seabirds, sea caves for choughs and woodland for the endangered red squirrel.

For centuries the seas around Anglesey have been a hazard to shipping, resulting in many shipwrecks and establishing the reputation of the island's lifeboatmen for their bravery. Despite its many visitors the island remains a stronghold of Welsh language and culture.

The 42 linked circular walks in this new revised edition explore the beautiful diverse landscape of the AONB and its fascinating history. The walks include the best sections of the Coastal Path and the island's high viewpoints. They pass lighthouses and beacons installed in the 19th C to help protect shipping. They feature old telegraph stations, ancient churches, impressive Neolithic burial chambers, Iron Age hillforts, old brickworks, Holy Wells, a country park and historic communities. Also included is Parys Mountain, once the world's major source of copper and the nearby historic port of Amlwch.

The routes, which range from a 2¼ mile Copper Mine Trail to a 10½ mile exploration of Holy Island, are well within the capability of most people. Many routes contain shorter walk options. A key feature is that individual walks can easily be linked with others to provide longer and more challenging day walks if required. They follow public rights of way or permissive paths, and cross Open Access land. Walking boots are recommended, along with appropriate clothing to protect against the elements. Please remember that the condition of the paths can vary according to season and weather! Contact the Isle of Anglesey County Council regarding any problems encountered (see page 44 for details).

Each walk has a detailed map and description which enables the route to be followed without difficulty, but be aware that changes in detail can occur at any time. The location of each walk is shown on the back cover and a summary of the key features of each is provided. This includes an estimated walking time, but allow more time to enjoy the scenery. Many walks are accessible by local bus services.

Please observe the country code and respect any ancient site visited. Enjoy your walking!

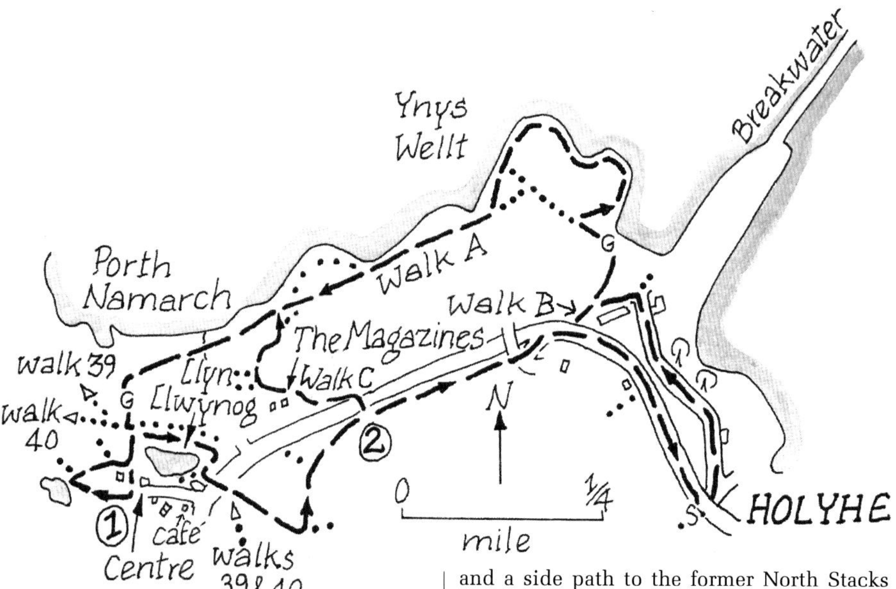

WALK 1

BREAKWATER COUNTRY PARK

DESCRIPTION A 2½ mile **(A)**, 2 mile **(B)** or 1½ mile **(C)** walk around the Park, featuring two small lakes, a section of Coastal Path (CP) and remnants of its quarrying past. Allow about 1½ hours.

START Holyhead Breakwater Country Park Information Centre [SH 226833].

DIRECTIONS The Country Park lies beneath Holyhead Mountain and is signposted from the northern end of Holyhead.

***The Country Park** opened in 1990 on the site of the former quarry which produced rock for the foundation of Holyhead's impressive breakwater – the longest in Europe, built between 1846-73 and which helped Holyhead develop as a major passenger and commercial port, with regular large ferry traffic to Ireland. The site was later used for brickmaking, then closed in the 1970s. It's attractions include industrial artefacts, a small lake, an outside gallery and a café.*

1 From the Information Centre entrance take the signposted Nature Trail diagonally opposite. Follow the trail past the Top Lake and a side path to the former North Stacks fog cannon. Turn RIGHT to a finger post, then LEFT past the end of nearby Llyn Llwynog. Go along the lake's northern side and round past its end, then take a path on the left to pass a small reservoir. Cross the road to signposted paths opposite. Go up the left fork (Holyhead), then turn LEFT down a hedge-lined bridleway. (Shortly, for **Walk C**, cross a bridge over the adjoining road then follow the path past The Magazines. At a path junction follow a waymarked path right down to join the Coastal Path.)

2 Continue on the bridleway, then a track down to the road. Follow it past an old works entrance providing access to the nearby Coastal Path (**Walk B**). Take the second signed path on the right down to a stile. Go under the road bridge, then bear LEFT up a road to pass two former hotels. *The second castellated one was originally built in 1848 as residence for the engineer responsible for the harbour developments.* At its end follow the signposted CP LEFT along a wide stony track, then at the far end of the former engine sheds RIGHT down to the pebbly shore, then shore, then LEFT up to a kissing gate. At a path junction follow the waymarked CP around Ynys Wellt then along the coast – *with a view of the former North Stack Fog Signal Station.* Later it bends inland to a kissing gate and a stony track. Turn LEFT to a nearby entrance accessing the lake and car park.

1 Walk through and out of the village. After Western Heights take a signposted path down a track angling right. Follow it across estate land into woodland leading to Carreglwyd. Briefly keep with the left fork, then turn LEFT through a gate and RIGHT along another stony track through trees and across open country. *On a nearby hill is the ruin of a telegraph station, part of a communications system built in 1826/7 to monitor shipping between Holyhead and Liverpool. In 1836 it was replaced by a new one further north.*

2 At conifer trees you have a choice to point 3: **Route (a)**: cross a stone stile on the left, follow the field path down to a road. Follow it RIGHT. **Route (b)**: go through the adjoining gate and follow the wall on your right along the long field towards a distant ruined windmill down to cross a stream and two ladder-stiles. Angle LEFT to follow the boundary to a kissing gate just beyond a house. Follow its access track to the road.

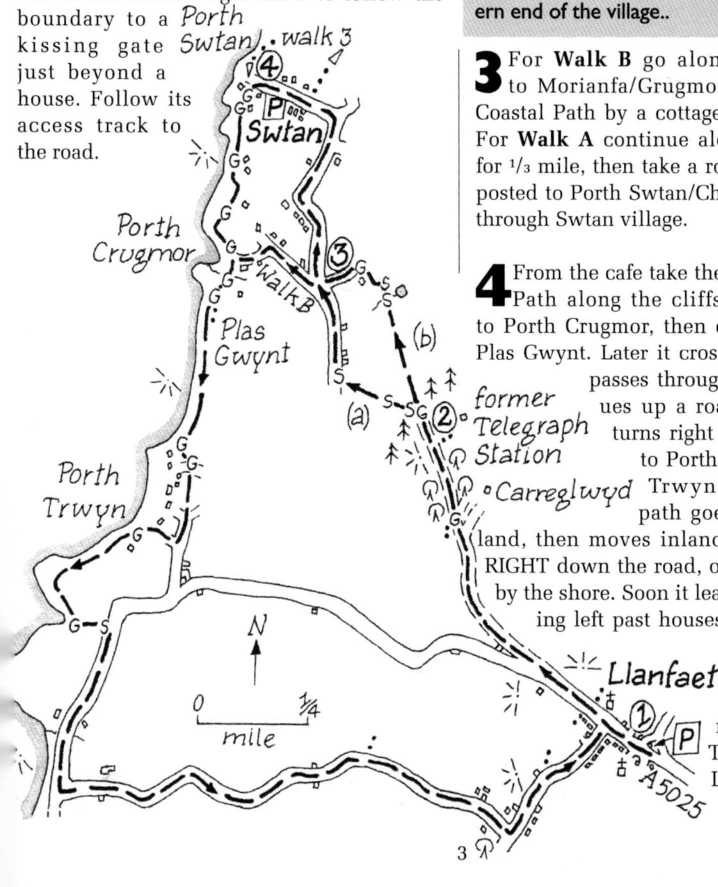

WALK 2

PORTH SWTAN & PORTH TRWYN

DESCRIPTION A 5¼ mile walk (**A**) exploring the attractive countryside and coast between Llanfaethlu and Swtan. The route passes a ruined telegraph station on its way to popular Porth Swtan (Church Bay), with its interesting thatched heritage museum, recommended Wavecrest café (*closed Mon-Wed*) and Lobster Pot restaurant. It then follows the Coastal Path (CP) south along low cliffs (some National Trust owned), before returning by quiet country lane. Allow about 3 hours. A 4½ mile walk (**B**) to Porth Crugmor is included.

START Llanfaethlu [SH 869315] or Swtan [SH 891301].

DIRECTIONS Llanfaethlu adjoins the A5025. There is a small car park on entering the southern end of the village..

3 For **Walk B** go along the minor road to Morianfa/Grugmor Fawr to join the Coastal Path by a cottage at Porth Crugmor. For **Walk A** continue along the road north for 1/3 mile, then take a road on the left signposted to Porth Swtan/Church Bay. Follow it through Swtan village.

4 From the cafe take the signposted Coastal Path along the cliffs, later descending to Porth Crugmor, then continuing through Plas Gwynt. Later it crosses an access track, passes through gorse and continues up a road. Shortly, the CP turns right along a stony track to Porth Trwyn, then enters Trwyn-Gwter-fudr. The path goes across the headland, then moves inland to the road. Turn RIGHT down the road, over a bridge and on by the shore. Soon it leaves the CP by bending left past houses. Follow the attractive meandering minor road for a further mile to a T-junction. Turn LEFT into Llanfaethlu.

WALK 3

PORTH SWTAN & MYNYDD Y GARN

DESCRIPTION A 6¼ mile walk of contrasting coastal and rural scenery. After reaching the shore it follows the Coastal Path south along the cliffs past popular Porth Swtan (Church Bay) to Swtan, with its interesting thatched heritage museum, recommended Wavecrest café (*closed Mon-Wed*) and Lobster Pot restaurant. The return by quiet lanes and field paths passes near the Church Bay Inn and features a short climb onto Mynydd y Garn (558 feet/170 metres), owned by the National Trust, for panoramic views across Anglesey. Allow about 3½ hours.

START National Trust Mynachdy car park [SH 303914] or Swtan [SH 891301].

DIRECTIONS Turn off the A5025 to Llanfairynghornwy. Go through the village, past a turn on the left, then a no through road on the right to find the National Trust car park on the right at a bend. It can also be accessed from the south.

1 Follow the track to the nearby kissing gate/gate. Continue with the signposted Coast Path along the track. When it bends half-right go straight ahead on a waymarked path to stiles at a stony track. Keep ahead across open ground parallel with a nearby stony track, soon descending onto a lower level. Continue ahead down to a waymarker post, then go along the narrowing field to a waymarker post at an old field boundary beneath a nearby brick building. Continue down the field edge then green and stony track to the shore by Llyn y Fydlyn. *Nearby is Ynys y Fydlyn sea arch.*

2 At the fence corner turn LEFT and climb up the slope to a kissing gate, then to the top of the cliffs. Follow the waymarked Coastal Path along the cliffs – *enjoying extensive views along the coast to Holyhead and the Lleyn peninsula beyond. You might see ferries on their way to or back from Ireland.* Shortly it descends then continues along the cliffs, later entering Clegir Mawr, owned by the National Trust. It then passes above Porth Swtan to reach the road at Swtan, where the nearby Wavecrest café serving home made food makes a great break.

3 Go up the road through the village, then take a signposted path through a kissing gate on the left opposite Ty Newydd. Follow the path to a road by Gadlys. Continue up the road ahead to a junction by the church. (For the nearby Church Bay Inn turn right.) Go up the road ahead – *soon with views south from Holyhead Mountain to Snowdonia.* At the junction bear LEFT up past Gray Rocks. At the next junction turn RIGHT heading towards Mynydd y Garn with its monument. After passing Aelwyd Uchaf Mon go through a kissing gate on the right. After a few yards head half-LEFT up the field, through a wall gap and on beneath Mynydd y Garn to a kissing gate in the boundary corner into National Trust land. Take a path leading RIGHT up to the monument and trig point on the top of Mynydd y Garn for panoramic views across Anglesey. *The stone obelisk was erected in 1897 to commemorate Sir William Thomas (1836-1915). Born in nearby Llanrhuddlad he became a successful shipowner in Liverpool, Mayor of Bootle and in 1897 High Sheriff of Anglesey.* Return down the path, then turn RIGHT along another path to a stile/gate. Keep ahead to a kissing gate. Continue to a stone stile in the wall corner ahead.

4 Follow the boundary on your left then go down the right-hand edge of the long narrow field. At the bottom take a path leading RIGHT into the nearby field then turn LEFT along its edge to a stile onto a road. Turn RIGHT past Waen Lydon, then take a signposted enclosed path on the left. Soon cross a ladder-stile on the right. Angle slightly LEFT across the field down to a ladder-stile in the boundary corner. Here turn LEFT across the field down to a gate in the fence. Go across the next field to a ladder-stile at Pendref smallholding ahead. Follow its access track to a gate to join a stony track beyond. Follow it LEFT to the road. Follow it RIGHT to Mynachdy car park.

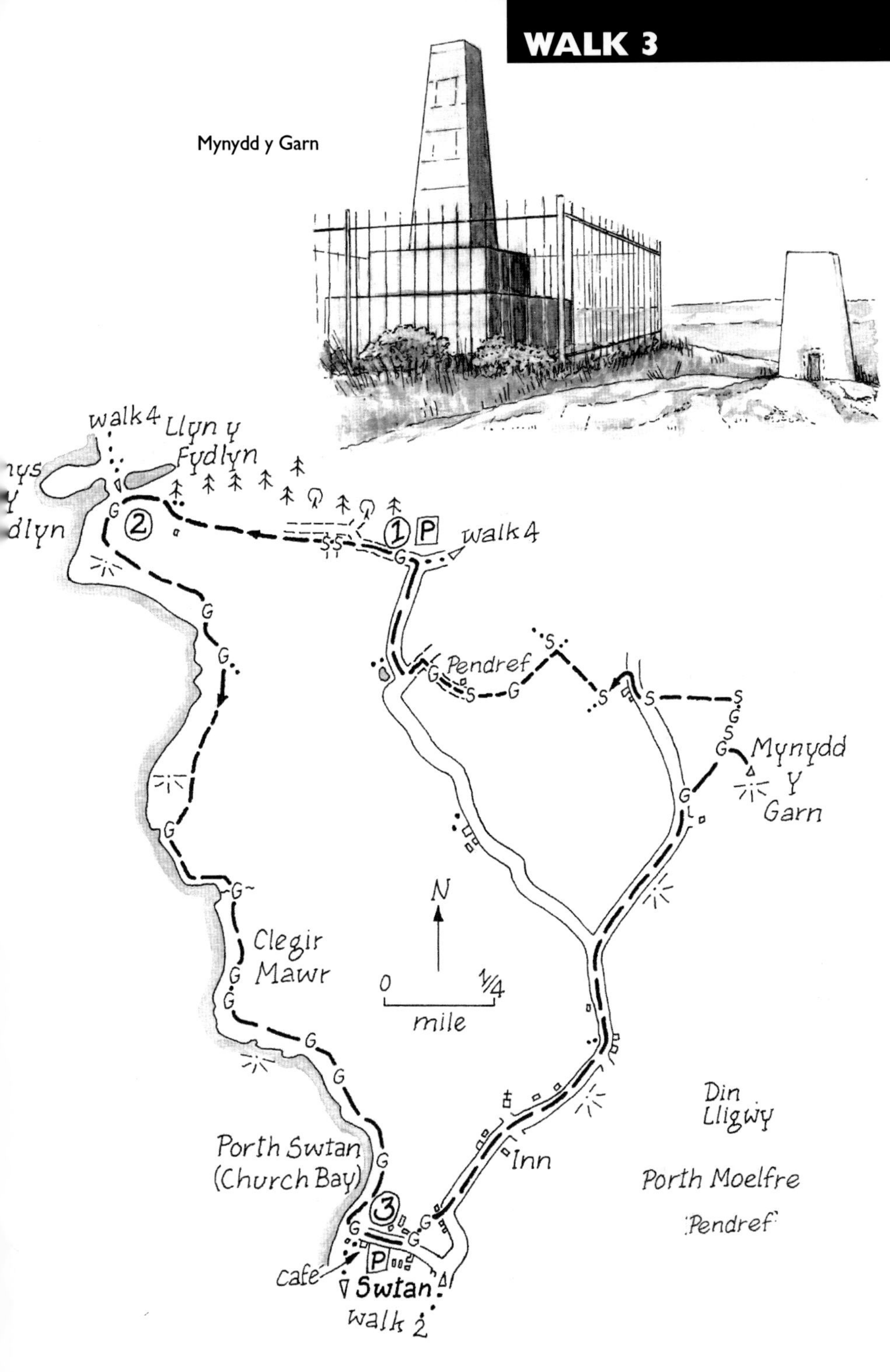

Mynydd y Garn

WALK 4

CARMEL HEAD

DESCRIPTION A 5 mile walk (**A**) across country to Hen Borth then following the Coastal Path around Carmel Head, part of the Mynachdy estate owned by the National Trust. It visits the 'White Ladies' pilot beacons and 19thC copper mine chimney, and reaches a high viewpoint above Porth yr Hwch. The more rugged undulating next section of the Coastal Path to Llyn y Fydlyn is only open 1 Feb -14 Sept. Allow about 3½ hours. An alternative attractive 3½ mile walk (**B**) is included.

START National Trust Mynachdy car park [SH 303914].

DIRECTIONS See Walk 3.

The sea off Carmel Head*, the remote north-western tip of Anglesey, with its submerged rocks, treacherous currents, and small islands, is among the most dangerous in Britain, resulting in many shipwrecks. In 1716, as an aid to navigation, a private entrepreneur built a coal beacon on The Skerries, a long island lying in the shipping lane between Liverpool and Ireland. It was replaced by a new lighthouse with oil lamps and reflectors in 1804. It was the last privately owned lighthouse in Britain when it was sold Trinity House in 1841. The light was automated in 1987. In the 1860s, two large white triangular stone pillars, known as the 'White Ladies' were erected on the headland. When aligned with a third marker on West Mouse island they provided an exact bearing of Coal Rock, a hazard to shipping.*

1 Turn LEFT along the road down to a junction. Follow the no through road to enter the farmyard at Mynachdy. (For **Walk B** turn left and follow the waymarked path up a track past outbuildings, across open ground, then round the dam of a reedy reservoir up to a ladder-stile. Angle left to a stile/gate, then continue to a stile/gate near a ruin. Pass the higher of the 'White Ladies' ahead to join the Coastal Path at the old mine chimney. Now follow instructions from the third sentence in paragraph 2 up to point 3.) For **Walk A** turn RIGHT through a gate by outbuildings. Follow the short farm track, then a wide stony track to its end. Continue through the field on an old raised green track to a ladder-stile, then down a hedged-lined green track to Hen Felin. Follow its access track to a gate. Just beyond go through a kissing gate on the left. Follow the path to join the Coast Path at Hen Borth.

2 Follow the Coastal Path west through kissing gates to enter Mynachdy estate and eventually reach Carmel Head and the 'White Ladies'. After passing the lower pillar follow the waymarked path via a footbridge to the former copper mine chimney. Head west to a stile by a waymarked gatepost and a ruin, then ahead across the headland past a waymarker post. Later – *with a view of Holyhead Mountain* – take the higher of two paths on the left up to a waymarker post to the left of the rocky summit. Continue up to a prominent viewpoint overlooking Porth yr Hwch.

3 Follow the waymarked Coastal Path down to a kissing gate and another below. Here it rises RIGHT to the steep cliffs, and continues along a small heather-covered rocky ridge. It then descends and heads seawards, passing a tall concrete post. Shortly the cliff-top path passes the impressive sea arch of Ynys y Fydlyn then descends towards Llyn y Fydlyn and bends down to a kissing gate. At the next fence corner turn LEFT up a stony track, soon taking its right fork. Go up the right-hand field edge past a waymark post beneath a nearby brick building. Go ahead along a narrow field, at its end rising past a waymarker post

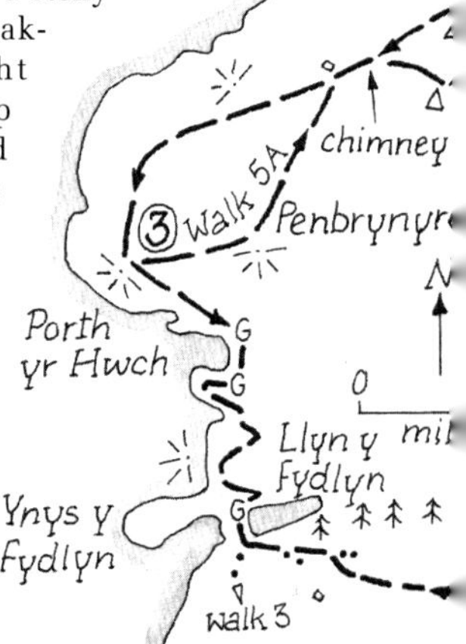

and continuing parallel with a nearby stony track. Go over a slight rise and on to stiles by a track. Continue to another stony track which takes you to the car park.

WALK 5

TRWYN CEMLYN & CARMEL HEAD

DESCRIPTION A 7 mile (**A**) or 6 mile (**B**) walk from Cemlyn Nature Reserve (for information see Walk 6) via Trwyn Cemlyn following the Coastal Path to the 'White Ladies' (for information see Walk 4) on Carmel Head. Walk A continues up to a good viewpoint, then the summit of Penbrynyreglwys, before joining Walk B for the return via Mynachdy and an ancient church. Allow about 4 hours. Also included is an easy 2¼ mile walk to the church (**C**).

START Cemlyn car park (west) [SH 329935].

DIRECTIONS Cemlyn is signposted from the A5025 at the Douglas Inn, Tregele. Take the second road on the right. At the lagoon take the next no through road right to a large car park at its end. Note it is liable to flooding at high tide.

1 Take the signposted Coastal Path along the track to Cemlyn Bay, then past a lifeboat commemorative monument. Follow a permissive path to the tip of Trwyn Cemlyn, returning south west above the shore – *with a view to Carmel Head and The Skerries lighthouse.* Follow the Coastal Path through kissing gates to eventually bend down to above Hen Borth. (For **Walk C** angle back across the field to the small 12thC church of St. Rhwydrus – *originally founded in the 6thC and dedicated to a little known saint from Ireland.* Afterwards head to the farm and go through the farmyard. Follow its access lane past the lagoon to a junction. Turn LEFT past Bryn Aber to the start.) For **Walks A/B** descend to Hen Borth's pebbly beach.

2 Follow instructions in paragraph 2 of Walk 4. (For **Walk B**, at the former 19thC copper mine chimney turn sharp left across the slope past the other pillar to a stone stile/gateway. Follow the faint track to another stile/gate. Angle right to a ladder-stile, then follow the track past the remains of a reedy reservoir and on to Mynachdy farm. In the

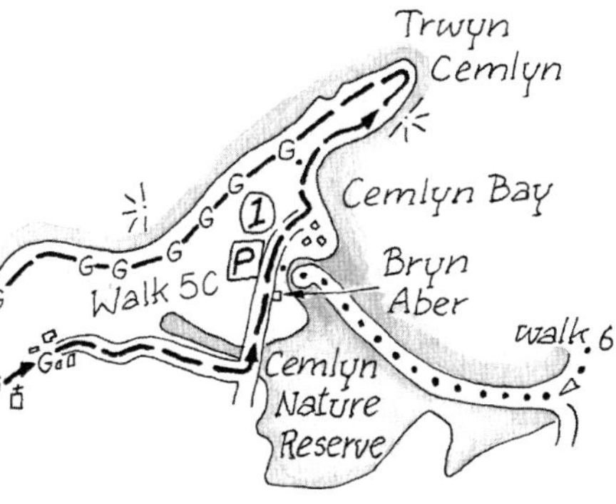

farmyard go through a gate ahead by outbuildings. Follow the farm track to a stile to join a wide stony track. which you follow to its end. Continue through the field on an old raised green track to a ladder-stile, then down a narrow hedged-lined green track to Hen Felin. Follow its access track to a gate. Just beyond go through a kissing gate on the left. Follow the path to join your outward route at Hen Borth. Shortly head over to the church and follow Walk C back.)

3 For **Walk A** head east and work your way up the small cairn on the top of Penbrynyreglwys. Go north a little further then head north east down towards the chimney to join Walk B for the return – see above.)

WALK 6

CEMLYN NATURE RESERVE

DESCRIPTION A 5¼ mile walk featuring a section of the Coastal Path (CP) and Cemlyn Nature Reserve. The route follows the Coastal Path through woodland near the former Wylfa power station, across country, then along the low cliffs to Cemlyn Nature Reserve. It then circuits the lagoon, before returning along the Coastal Path, then minor road. Allow about 3 hours. A simple 1½ mile circuit of the reserve can be made from car parks at either end.

START Car park, near Wylfa Power Station [SH 357937] or Cemlyn car park (east) [SH 336932].

DIRECTIONS On the bend of the A5025 between Cemaes and Tregele take a road leading north west. Just before Wylfa site entrance take the side road to the car park at its end. Cemlyn is signposted from the A5025 at Tregele.

***Cemlyn Nature Reserve**, owned by the National Trust, comprises a freshwater lagoon separated from the sea by a shingle ridge, except at high tide. It is one of the most important breeding sites for terns in Wales and attracts wildfowl in winter. The lagoon was created from salt marsh in the 1930's then managed as a wildfowl refuge by Capt. Vivian Hewitt, a pioneer aviator and dedicated ornithologist. He lived at nearby Bryn Aber, whose high walls built in 1939 created a sheltered garden for birds. You can walk along the lagoon outside the tern breeding season (April -July inclusive) and on the seaward side of the ridge during that breeding period.*

1 From the car park entrance follow the signposted Coastal Path almost opposite through the wood, shortly bending left up to a path junction. Turn LEFT up through the trees, down a zig-zag path, then under a pylon. Follow the path ahead, soon bending right and continuing to the wood end. Bear LEFT to join Wylfa site's access road's and walk along the pavement. After passing Wylfa Office Site entrance take the signposted CP opposite to a kissing gate/gate. The CP continues along a fenced path beside a track, alternating sides, then crossing its bend to a kissing gate ahead. After another kissing gate cross a track and follow the CP to the wood corner and down to a shoreline kissing gate. Cross the stone slab bridge by a large stone building and go up to a waymarked path junction. Follow the CP near the shore at Porth-y-pistyll, over heather/gorse covered Trwyn Pencarreg, then above Cemlyn Bay to eventually reach Cemlyn car park.

2 Walk along the shingle ridge, known as Esgair Gemlyn, to the road and car park. Follow the road south past Bryn Aber and over the causeway to a junction. Turn

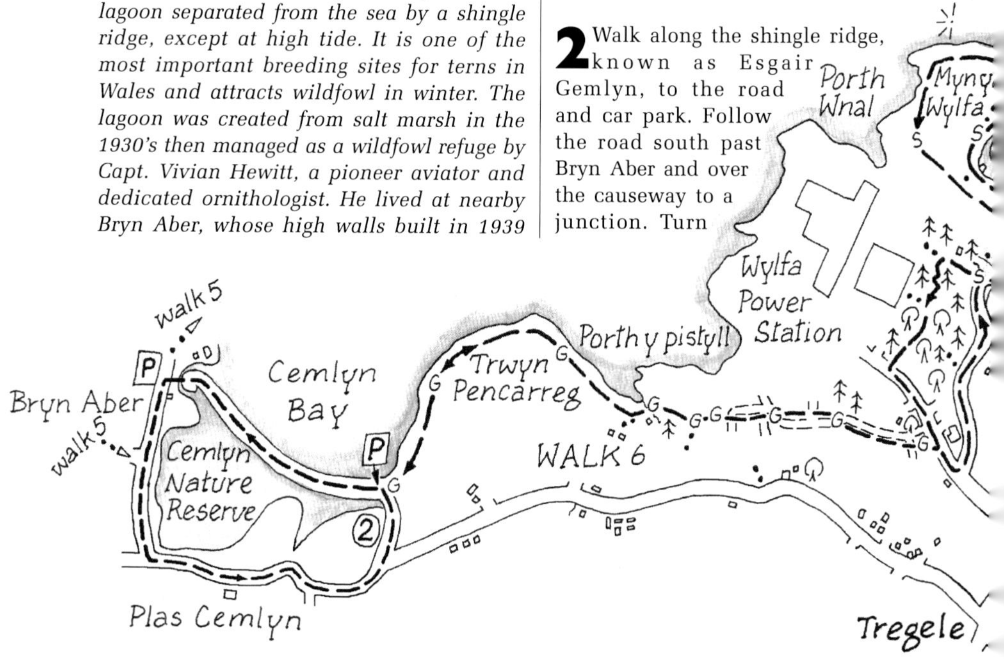

LEFT and follow roads as shown back to the Cemlyn car park. Return along the CP to Wylfa Site's access road. Follow it RIGHT then turn LEFT along the side road to the start.

WALK 7

WYLFA HEAD

DESCRIPTION A 4½ mile walk from the most northerly village in Wales, with its attractive sheltered harbour. It first heads inland along a wooded valley to visit old brickworks, then follows the Coastal Path (CP) around Mynydd y Wylfa headland, returning via field paths. Allow about 3 hours.

START Cemaes Bay beach car park [SH 373935].

DIRECTIONS At the bottom of the High Street turn right, cross the river to find the car park signposted. Small fee payable. Alternative large free village car behind High Street, which route passes.

1 From the car park cafe take the signposted Coastal Path above the small sandy beach, soon bending inland above the river and passing under the road bridge. Follow the former tramway up the wooded valley signposted to the brickworks. At a path T-junction, turn RIGHT then LEFT under the road bridge by the river. Follow the path to the former brickworks (1907-1914). Retrace your steps then cross the footbridge over the river. Follow the path back along the river's tree-covered western bank. Just before the footbridge turn LEFT up to the village centre. Go down the High Street. At its end keep ahead on the road's right fork (signposted harbour/beach). Go past the entrance to the jetty and continue above the beach. At the pavement end bear RIGHT to follow the signposted CP up between houses, then RIGHT between walls onto the cliffs by Angorfa. Continue along the waymarked cliff-top CP, around Porth Wylfa, then on above Porth yr Ogof to enter Mynydd y Wylfa.

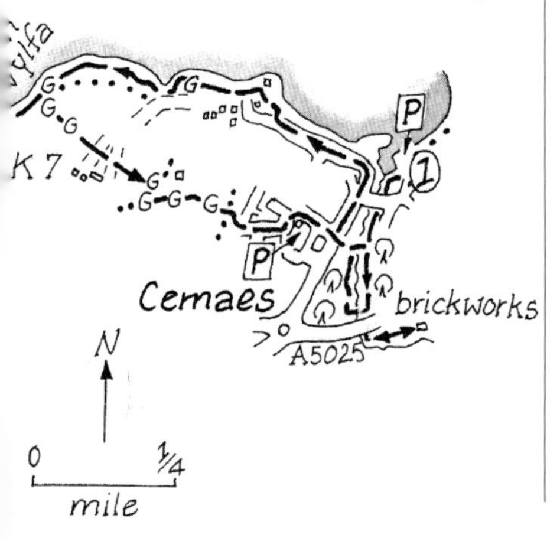

2 Follow the path leading RIGHT to the rocky north eastern corner of Wylfa Head. Now head west with the cliff-top path past a former lookout station – *with good views to Carmel Head, the Skerries, and nearby Wylfa nuclear power station, which generated electricity from 1971 until December 2015. Its decommissioning will take some years. A new nuclear power plant is being planned.* At the headland's north western tip, follow the cliff-top path south towards Wylfa and on to a stile/gate in the wall ahead. Go along the field edge and through a nearby waymarked old gateway. Go along the next field edge to a kissing gate on the right. Follow the waymarked CP, soon descending through trees to a track leading to nearby gates, with a car park visible ahead.

3 Follow a path angling LEFT through trees past a wall then across a large field to a familiar kissing gate. Now follow your outward route past Porth Wylfa, then go through a kissing gate on the right. Go through two fields, across two tracks, then along a field edge to a kissing gate onto a waymarked cross-path. Turn RIGHT to a nearby kissing gate, then LEFT along the edge of two fields through kissing gates, then along a short enclosed path to a stony cross-path. Turn RIGHT then LEFT up another path to a road. Go up the road ahead. At a T-junction turn LEFT. On the bend take a path angling down on the right past the library. Follow the road past the car park to the High Street. Follow your outward route opposite down to cross the footbridge and back to the start.

WALK 8

PORTH LLANLLEIANA & LLANBADRIG CHURCH

DESCRIPTION A 3¾ mile walk through attractive countryside to former porcelain works at Porth Llanlleaina. It then returns along the stunning cliff-top Coastal Path via ancient Llanbadrig Church. Allow about 2½ hours. An alternative 2 mile walk is to follow the road up to the church and return along the Coastal Path.
START Cemaes Bay beach car park [SH 376937] or [SH 373935].
DIRECTIONS The car park (also Llanbadrig church/Gadlys Hotel) is signposted off the A5025 just east of Cemaes. For the alternative beach car park (fee) see Walk 7.

***Llanbadrig church**, founded in 440 AD, is the only church in Wales dedicated to St Patrick of Ireland, allegedly after he sheltered in a cave here following being shipwrecked. The current church, in its dramatic cliff-top setting, dates from the 12thC with later renovations and additions.*

1 Go back up the road to the junction. Turn RIGHT then then take a signposted enclosed path over a stone stile on the left to a kissing gate. Continue with the path beneath the bracken-covered slope, then across a small field to gates in the corner. Go along the next field edge to gates, then along the lawn edge of a nearby house and over its access track to a small gate. Follow the path through the field ahead, a boundary gap, and another field down to a footbridge/small gate, then up to a road.

2 Follow it RIGHT. When the road bends right take a signposted path through a kissing gate on the left. Go up and along the field edge following the telegraph poles and over the stony access track leading to Llanlleiana. Go down the narrow green track ahead, then a field towards Dinas Gynfor and across a causeway over a reedy marsh. Just beyond an old gateway/concrete ladder-stile you join the Coastal Path. Follow it LEFT to reach the ruins and chimney of the former Llanlleiana porcelain works – *which used china clay from Dinas Gynfor until it closed in 1920.*

3 Follow the Coastal Path up steps and through a small gate. The path now rises in stages along the cliffs. After an undulating section of cliff-top path, you go through two kissing gates at a good viewpoint. Continue with the undulating path. After another kissing gate the path continues along the top of impressive vertical cliffs, then beside the graveyard wall of Llanbadrig church. After a small gate at its corner go up the slope ahead past a seat and down to a cross-path. Follow it to the tip of the headland, then return along its south side, rising above Porth Padrig, then bending left to a small gate into a small car-park by the church. After visiting the church go down the road and through a kissing gate to follow the cliff-top Coastal Path to the start.

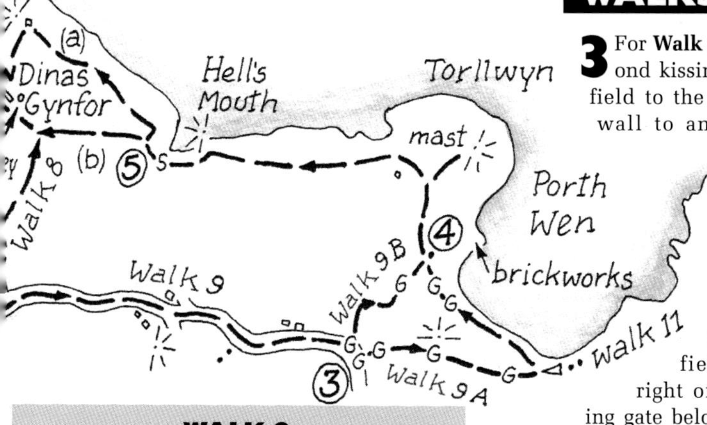

WALK 9

PORTH WEN & DINAS GYNFOR

DESCRIPTION An exhilarating 6½ mile (**A**) or 6 mile (**B**) walk featuring one of Anglesey's best sections of rugged high cliffs, offering extensive coastal views. The outward route passes through attractive countryside then offers a choice of paths to Porth Wen, with Walk A offering the better views of the impressive old shoreline brickworks and sea arch. In the early 20thC clay from nearby cliffs was used in 3 beehive kilns to make silica bricks for the steel industry and shipped from the small quay. It closed in 1924. The return route, following the undulating cliff-top Coastal Path, features Dinas Gynfor with its Iron Age Hillfort and the remains of Llanlleiana porcelain works and the ancient Llanbadrig Church. Allow about 4 hours.
START As Walk 8.

1 Go Follow instructions in paragraph 1 of Walk 8.

2 Turn RIGHT along the road, later rising steadily to a 1902 chapel at its highest point. Eventually you reach two signposted paths on the left. For **Walk B** take the first one through a kissing gate, by a gate. Follow the enclosed path, soon bending down towards Porth Wen. After a kissing gate continue down the wide path to a waymark post at a crossroad of paths overlooking the chimneys of the old brickworks at point 4.

3 For **Walk A** go through the second kissing gate and along the field to the left of an old stone wall to another kissing gate. Angle RIGHT across the next field and down to a kissing gate – *with the first view of Porth Wen, the old brickworks and sea arch.* Go ahead down the field, passing to the right of boulders to a kissing gate below. Turn LEFT a few yards, then RIGHT along a narrow cross-path down through gorse/bracken, to join the wide Coastal Path. Turn LEFT. Follow the Coastal Path up past Porth Wen to a kissing gate. Continue to another kissing gate and on up to a waymark post at a crossroad of paths.

4 Follow the wide Coastal Path rising steadily towards a mast on Torllwyn headland. Take the right fork up past the mast to a great viewpoint. Return to the Coastal Path. Follow it past an old winding house, then along the heather/bracken covered undercliff and a section of near vertical cliffs. After a good viewpoint to the tower on Dinas Gynfor the path then begins a long steady descent to Hell's Mouth. Go up the stepped path.

5 At the waymarked path junction you have a choice of routes to the former Llanlleiana porcelain works: Recommended Route (**a**): turn RIGHT – *with a good view back along vertical cliffs* – and climb steadily to the top of Dinas Gynfor and on to the small tower – *built to commemorate Edward VII's coronation in 1901 and offering views to the lighthouse on the Skerries. Ramparts of the hillfort can be seen on the inland side.* Soon the path descends steeply. Route (**b**): keep ahead with the waymarked path, soon angling down the bracken-covered hillside. At a path junction bear RIGHT. *The porcelain works used China clay from the hillside, and the tiny cove for shipping during the 19thC until its closure in 1920.* Now follow instructions in paragraph 3 of Walk 8.

WALK 10

PORTH WEN

DESCRIPTION An interesting 3½ mile walk from Bull Bay. The route follows the delightful cliff-top Coastal Path to Porth Wen to view the well preserved old brickworks on the western side of this attractive bay. It then returns on tracks and field paths via a ruined windmill. Allow about 2 hours.

START Bull Bay [SH 426943].

DIRECTIONS At Bull Bay turn off the bend of the A5025 to the shore. Roadside parking or signposted village car park.

1 At the road junction by the Bull Bay Hotel take the surfaced Coastal Path below the 'Old Post Office', above the shore and along the cliffs to a kissing gate. Turn RIGHT along a lane to a stone stile at its end. Follow the Coastal Path along the top of the cliffs passing through kissing gates. Eventually you reach Porth Wen with a view of the old brickworks. *In the early 20thC material from nearby cliffs was used in three beehive kilns to make silica bricks for the steel industry and shipped from the small quay. It closed in 1924.* The path turns south along the eastern side of the bay later reaching a signposted path junction at a track just before Castell farm.

2 Turn LEFT up the track to reach three dwellings, then continue along their access lane. At a junction, turn LEFT along a track leading to Yr Erw. Cross a ladder-stile opposite its gated entrance. Go up the left-hand field edge to a waymark post just before the corner. Follow the enclosed path to a ladder-stile, then on to enter a field. Go along the field edge to a waymark post ahead, then go down an enclosed path and continue to a gate. Follow the path ahead up to a house. Go through three gates, then angle LEFT to a gate in the corner. *Amongst the buildings is a ruined windmill.* Bear RIGHT then LEFT past a small outbuilding to go through a gate on the right, Turn LEFT and follow the waymarked path onto a small gorse-covered ridge and down to a kissing gate.

3 Continue up the waymarked path to a post, then down the slope, at the bottom bending left to a waymark post at a wall end. Here turn RIGHT along the field edge to a kissing gate in the corner beneath Glaslyn to reach its driveway beyond. Go through the small gate opposite and follow the path to a kissing gate and across the next field to another kissing gate. Turn RIGHT along the stony access track. Shortly, cross a stile on the left and go down the field edge to a kissing gate. Descend steps and follow the enclosed path to a driveway by Bryn Arthur. Follow it down to the road in Bull Bay. Turn LEFT back to the start.

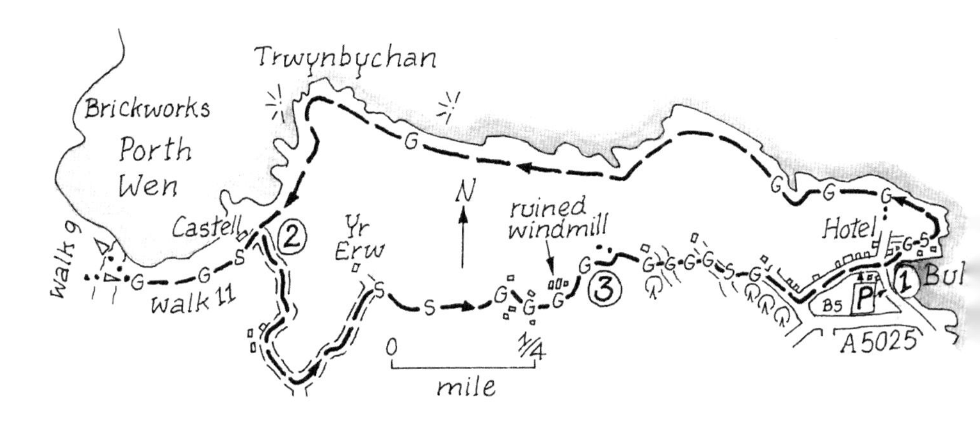

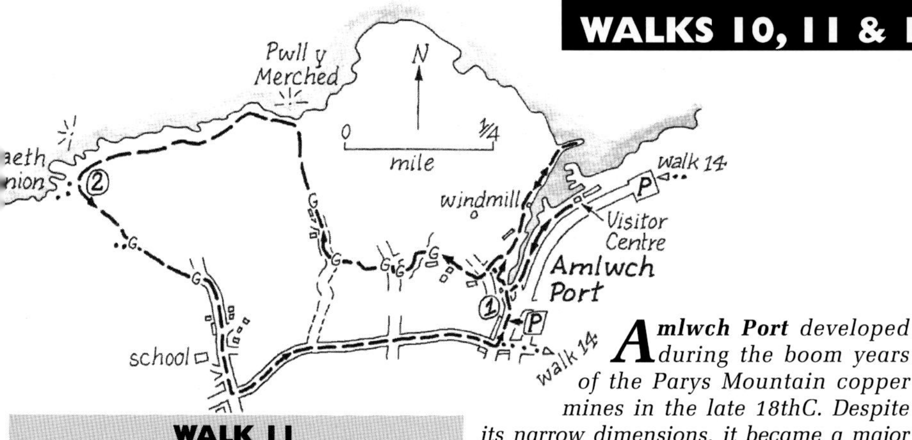

Amlwch Port developed during the boom years of the Parys Mountain copper mines in the late 18thC. Despite its narrow dimensions, it became a major port in Wales, exporting copper ore and importing scrap metal, used in copper extraction. It also had smelting and sulphur extraction works. As mining declined during the 19thC shipbuilding developed. The Copper Kingdom Centre's displays tell the area's copper mining industry, while the Visitor Centre has an interesting exhibition and café.

1 Go down the side road on the left then follow the Coastal Path on the right down to the quayside, and along the road past the Copper Kingdom Centre up to the Sail Loft Visitor Centre. Return to the side road near the start. Here follow the CP sharp RIGHT past a utility building and up to a stony track. Follow it RIGHT down and along the western side of the harbour, then paths to the jetty. Retrace your steps but continue up the track to a cross-track. Turn LEFT then RIGHT with the CP across a car park, then the park to a kissing gate – *note nearby windmill. Follow the path by a stream to a road.* Turn RIGHT along the pavement opposite to a small gate, then follow the CP across the old railway line and open ground to a kissing gate. Turn RIGHT along an enclosed track. When it splits keep ahead past Costog Fawr. Follow the walled path down to Pwll y Merched then continue along the cliff top path.

2 At a stepped railed path descending to rocks at Traeth Dynion follow an enclosed path inland to a road. Follow it RIGHT past a school to crossroads by the Library. Turn LEFT to follow the road to the start.

WALK 11

BULL BAY TO CEMAES BAY

DESCRIPTION An exhilarating 5 mile linear walk along a splendid section of the cliff top Coastal Path. Catch bus 61 from Cemaes to Bull Bay. Allow about 3½ hours.
START Bull Bay [SH 426943].

1 Follow instructions in paragraph 1 of Walk 10 to Castell farm.

2 Go past the house to a stile/gateway. Follow the waymarked Coastal Path across the field, up to a kissing gate and on to another kissing gate, soon joining Walk 9. Continue from the penultimate sentence in paragraph 3 in Walk 9 to Cemaes Bay.

WALK 12

TRAETH DYNION

DESCRIPTION A 3 mile walk combining an exploration of historic Amlwch Port with a short section of the Coastal Path (CP). Allow about 2 hours.
START Upper Quay Street car park, Amlwch Port [SH 449932].
DIRECTIONS From the roundabout on the A5025 at Amlwch, take the road signed for Amlwch Port/Copper Kingdom Centre, then its right fork. At the T-junction turn right. At the Liverpool Arms turn left to the car park and toilets.

WALK 13

PARYS MOUNTAIN TRAIL

DESCRIPTION A fascinating mile 2¼ mile waymarked Trail exploring this famous copper mine, developed by the Amlwch Industrial Heritage Trust. A detailed leaflet is available from a dispenser at the start. Allow about 1½ hours. The Trail follows stony tracks across an exposed site, so be prepared. Keep to the waymarked Trail and avoid any damage.

START Car park, Parys Mountain [SH 905437].

DIRECTIONS The car park is on the B5111 1¼ miles south from the A5025 roundabout at Amlwch.

***P**arys Mountain has been mined for copper by since prehistoric times, including during the Roman occupation. After large scale industrial extraction began in the mid 18thC, it became the world's major source of copper during the 1780s, employing several thousand men. Ore was initially mined from shallow shafts, then opencasts and finally from adits and deep shafts up to over 900 feet deep. Premium ore was shipped from Amlwch Port to South Wales or Lancashire for smelting. Other copper was extracted using kilns and furnaces, or through precipitation ponds. By-products such as ochre, sulphur and alum resulted in chemical industries developing on site.*

During the 19thC mining declined and deep mining ended in the 1880s. However it began again in the 1980s and continues today. The mountain's unusual landscape with its multi-coloured spoil heaps has been used in various films.

Windmill on Parys Mountain

1 Follow the track away from the car park, soon passing between pools and over a cross-track. It then bends down to a viewing platform and information board overlooking the impressive Great Opencast (1). The Trail continues past the remains of former offices, smithy and stores of Mona mine (2) then precipitation ponds (3). After passing a small lake it reaches a crossroad of tracks, the Trail turns LEFT and continues to the ruined Pearl Engine House (4) whose steam engine installed in 1819 pumped water from an adjoining shaft. The Trail continues its steady climb past a seat at a good viewpoint and Charlotte yard (5) where ore was broken up by women and roasted in kilns, to the windmill (6) on the summit. It was built in 1878 to pump water from the underground workings. Later after passing waste tips, the Trail bends left with the modern pithead winding gear now visible and descends to the road, before following a track up to join your outward route.

WALK 14

PORTH EILIAN

DESCRIPTION A 5½ mile (**A**) or 4½ mile (**B**) walk featuring contrasting rural and coastal scenery and a 19thC lighthouse. The route first passes through historic Amlwch Port, with its Visitor Centre, small harbour and Copper Kingdom Centre. It then follows roads and field paths to Porth Eilian, where Walk A extends to Point Lynas lighthouse, before returning along the cliff-top Coastal Path. Allow about 3½ hours. An alternative 3 mile walk (**C**) to Porthyrychen is included. The walk can be started from Upper Quay Street car park.

WALKS 13 & 14

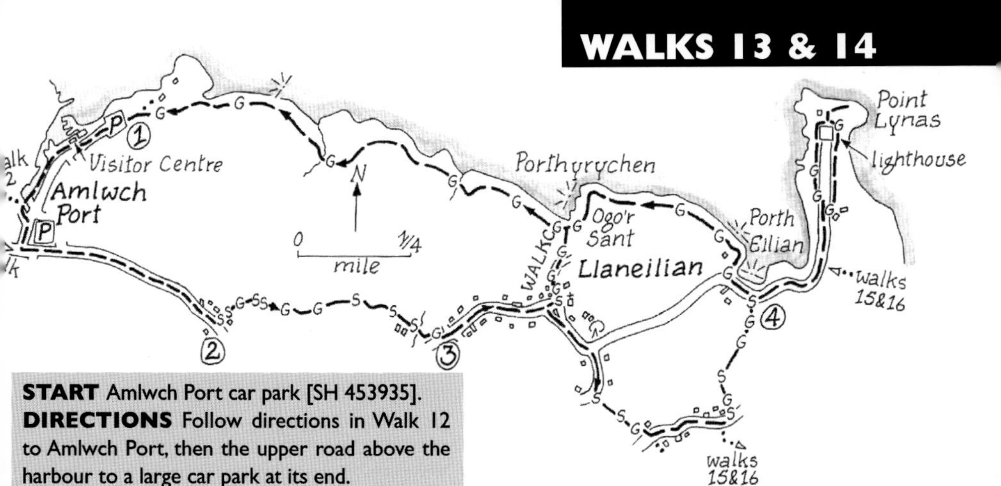

START Amlwch Port car park [SH 453935].
DIRECTIONS Follow directions in Walk 12 to Amlwch Port, then the upper road above the harbour to a large car park at its end.

Since the 18thC Point Lynas has provided assistance to passing ships trading with Liverpool. In 1781 a pilot station was established on the headland, from where pilots were taken by boat to join passing ships to guide them down the Mersey. The current building, comprising lamp room, telegraph and signal stations, was built in 1835 by Trustees of Liverpool Dock.

1 Return along the road then take the signposted Coastal Path down the side of Sail Loft Visitor Centre, containing café and exhibition, then down the road and past the Copper Kingdom Centre. Continue along the quayside, then follow the signposted Coastal Path to a road. Follow it up to Upper Quay Street car park. At the road junction by the Liverpool Arms turn LEFT up the road, later crossing to the pavement opposite, then grass verge just before leaving Amlwch.

2 About 100 yards after the road speed sign and just past Dolwen/Gorlan Hen, take a partly hidden signposted path over a stone stile on the left. Follow the enclosed path between houses to a stile and on to a small gate in the field corner. Go along the next field edge down to a stone stile, then across a small field to a stile ahead. Follow the enclosed path to a small gate and on through gorse/bracken to another small gate. Follow the path beside the wall to a stone stile, then across more open ground to a stile. Go across a small crop field to a wall by a house and on to a stile and footbridge over a stream. Go up the field to a waymark post and bear LEFT to a kissing gate in the corner.

3 Cross the road and follow it LEFT past Llaneillian WI Hall. (Shortly, for **Walk C** take a lane on the left past Plas Eilian to cross a stile by the church gate. Follow the signposted path to a gate and across the farmyard to a kissing gate/gate. Follow the waymarked path along an old track, through a gate then down the slope to join the Coastal Path between kissing gates below.) Continue along the road, then take the side road on the right to a stone stile/gate on its bend. Angle LEFT across two fields to another road. Follow it LEFT past houses to cross a stile and gate just beyond the last dwelling. Go down the field to a stile/gate in the corner. Turn RIGHT and walk along the edge of two fields (kissing gates), then an enclosed path to a road at Porth Eilian. (For **Walk B** turn LEFT.)

4 For the lighthouse turn RIGHT along the road. Later follow a waymarked path up round the lighthouse complex and down to rejoin the road. Follow it to the mini-roundabout at Porth Eilian. At the top of the slipway go through a small gate then follow the waymarked kissing gated Coastal Path along the cliffs past Porthyrychen. Later, the path moves inland through heather to cross a second footbridge, then returns to the cliffs, before bending towards Amlwch Port. It passes a derelict house, then follows a stony track to the car park.

WALK 15

MYNYDD EILIAN

DESCRIPTION A 7 mile (**A**) or 6½ mile (**B**) walk featuring one of Anglesey's high points, Mynydd Eilian (580 feet/177 metres), offering panoramic views, a splendid section of the Coastal Path, (CP) and 19thC Point Lynas lighthouse (See Walk 14 for information.). Allow about 4½ hours.

START Llaneilian car park [SH 474929].

DIRECTIONS The car park is on the right just before the road descends to the bay.

1 Go down the road past toilets to a mini-roundabout at Porth Eilian. Turn RIGHT along the road past a good view to Point Lynas lighthouse. Just before a cattle grid take a signposted path on the right to a stone stile. Follow the path to a kissing gate, along the field edge, keeping ahead at the corner to a hidden kissing gate. Go along the next field edge to a stile/gate, then up the next field to a minor road. Turn RIGHT over a cattle grip, then immediately LEFT up a signposted enclosed path, past the entrance to Coed Avens, then continue up an access track to a signposted crossroad of paths by an old barn.

2 Take the path up steps on the right and on past a large wall to a small gate. Go across the open hillside to a small gate and another ahead, then on to a kissing gate and up a house's access drive. Go along the road, soon descending, then go through a kissing gate up on the left. The path rises by the fence then bends right across the hillside, briefly rises then follow a boundary to a kissing gate. Cross the nearby ladder-stile, then follow the path up to a trig point on the top of Mynydd Eilian. Retrace your steps then continue down the path to a stone stile onto a road. Turn LEFT up the road. It later bends more south east and passes the driveway to Cae Ffynnon Wen by a cottage on the right. As the road bends half-right and rises towards houses, go through a gate on the left by an old finger post. Go half-RIGHT off the stony track past a telegraph pole to a gate. Continue in the same direction across the next field to a telegraph pole by a wood onto a road. Follow it LEFT past Tyddyn Mawr to a junction. Turn RIGHT towards Llys Dulas. (Later, for **Walk B** take the signposted path along the access track to Rhos-mynach-isaf, from where the path descends to join the Coastal Path at point 4.)

3 At Mulberry House by a road/track junction you join the Coastal Path. Cross the ladder-stile and continue beside the wall to two further ladder-stiles. Pass to the left of a telegraph pole ahead, then descend to a ladder-stile. Follow the path along the edge of three fields to reach Porth yr Aber, with the tower on Ynys Dulas ahead – *built in 1824 as a refuge for shipwrecked sailors, stocked with food and water.* Turn LEFT along the field edge round to a footbridge and kissing gate. Walk up the edge of the large field round to a kissing gate.

4 Continue with the waymarked CP, later descending to a kissing gate. The CP now moves further inland, guided by waymark posts, shortly rising steadily, then continues northwards – *shortly with a view of Point Lynas lighthouse and Freshwater Bay.* After crossing a stream the CP rises to a kissing gate. After a kissing gate and stile it continues to a kissing gate, where you are joined by Walk 16.

5 Follow the CP to a kissing gate, across the field, soon bending to another kissing gate and continuing west to a road. For the lighthouse turn RIGHT, through large gateposts and past a bungalow, then go through a kissing gate on the left. Follow the waymarked path up and round to the front of the lighthouse, then visit a small viewing platform at the tip of Point Lynas. Return along the waymarked path along the other side of the complex and down to a kissing gate to rejoin the road. Follow it back to the start.

Former telegraph station

WALK 16
POINT LYNAS

DESCRIPTION A 2¾ mile walk following waymarked paths up to the former 19thC telegraph station offering extensive views, then descending to join a short section of Coastal Path, before visiting 19thC Point Lynas lighthouse (See Walk 14 for information.) Allow about 2 hours.

START As Walk 15..

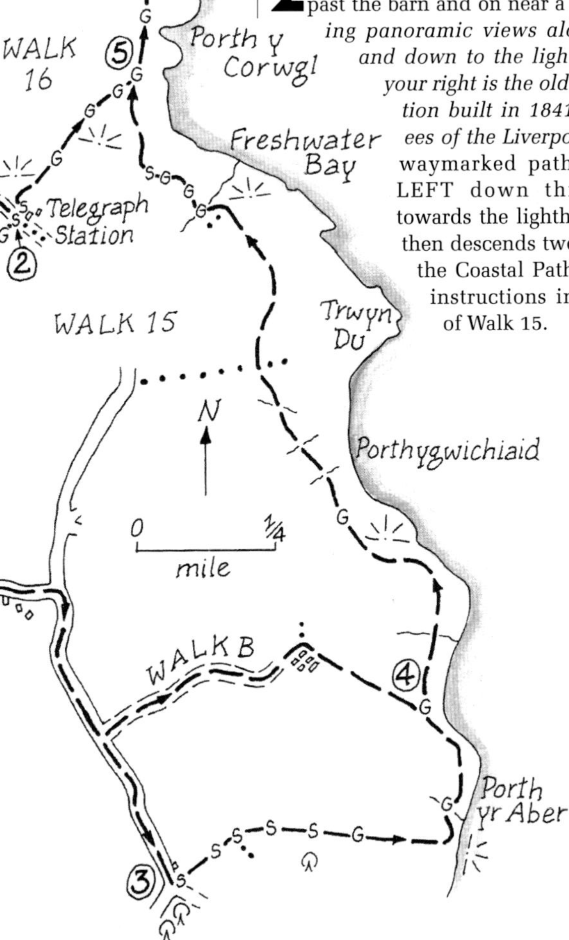

1 Follow instructions in paragraph 1 of Walk 15.

2 Turn LEFT over a stile. Follow the path past the barn and on near a fence – *enjoying panoramic views along the coast and down to the lighthouse. Up to your right is the old telegraph station built in 1841 by the trustees of the Liverpool Docks.* The waymarked path now angles LEFT down through gorse towards the lighthouse to a gate then descends two fields to join the Coastal Path. Now follow instructions in paragraph 5 of Walk 15.

WALK 17

MYNYDD BODAFON

DESCRIPTION A 7 mile walk featuring fine coastal scenery and panoramic views from an attractive small Open Access heathland hill, with refreshment options on route. It follows the Coastal Path (CP) to Traeth yr Ora, then inland via field paths to the Pilot Boat Inn and on to the summit of Mynydd Bodafon (584 feet/178 metres). It then returns via Brynrefail, with its tea-room. Allow about 4 hours.

START Lligwy Beach car park [SH 493873] or Brynrefail car park [SH 481869].

DIRECTIONS The beach car park is reached by minor roads from the A5025 at Brynrefail, opposite the alternative small car park at the northern end of the village..

1 From the car park's corner by the beach and a warning sign, follow the Coastal Path along the bracken and shrub-covered cliffs – *with a good view across Lligwy beach to the Great Orme* – to a kissing gate, and on past an old lookout tower to a good viewpoint. *On the small rock of Ynys Dulas is a distinctive tower built in 1824 as a refuge for shipwrecked sailors, stocked with food and water.* The CP then descends to a waymarked path junction, crosses the small sandy beach, then continues along the low cliffs to a second kissing gate above Traeth yr Ora.

2 Soon afterwards, at a waymarked path junction by a seat and kissing gate, turn LEFT up the tree-lined CP to cottages. Go up their access track. At a gate and lane, the CP goes through a kissing-gate almost opposite, then up the field to another by cottages. Continue up the field edge, then at a waymark post by a fence corner turn LEFT up through a gap in trees. The CP continues between boundaries, then goes up a field edge past a waymarked fence corner, with a ladder-stile on the left. Go up the field – *soon with a good view of Mynydd Bodafon* – and on past a small pool to follow the boundary to a kissing-gate/gate. Continue along the hedge-lined path to a kissing gate, then along the next large field edge to the Pilot Boat Inn.

3 Go past its end and follow the waymarked CP along the pavement by the A5025. When it turns right along a track continue along the roadside path. After the City Dulas road sign, cross the road with care to take a waymarked path up Tyddyn Bach's access track, then by the boundary to a small gate onto a side track. Turn RIGHT to rejoin Tyddyn Bach's access track. At the entrance to the cottage go through a small gate and follow the waymarked enclosed path round to a stile. Turn RIGHT along the field edge to a stile, then go along the next. At a waymark post turn LEFT up the field by a ditch, later crossing a footbridge over it to a nearby footbridge and stile. Bear RIGHT to follow a part boardwalked path (can be muddy) to a stile by a ruined farm. Follow the waymarked path to cross a nearby footbridge, then LEFT up above the stream, soon angling away up through gorse to a ladder-stile. The waymarked path now bears LEFT up the field edge to another hidden ladder-stile and a small gate beyond. Continue up the field edge to another small gate in the corner – *with good views to Holyhead and Parys Mountains.* Now go up the edge of three fields to a gate, then an enclosed path to a ladder-stile. Angle across to a waymarked gateway then follow the fence to a small gate to join a green track beyond. Follow it LEFT and go along a short section of stony track.

4 Just before it splits near Salem and Ty Uchaf, turn RIGHT along a waymarked path rising across gorse and heather towards the trig point on Mynydd Bodafon, After a cross-path it levels out and reaches a path junction (the path on the left is your return). Follow the path ahead, soon narrowing, down through gorse and bracken past a nearby cottage to a stony track. Follow it LEFT for about 25 yards, then turn LEFT across a stony parking area. Now follow a good path up to the trig point on the top of Mynydd Bodafon. Follow a path from its other side down the rocky slope. At a path T-junction take the path leading left down through bracken and gorse to join your outward route visible ahead. Return to the tracks at point 4. Follow the waymarked path along the left track between cottages to a ladder-stile at Caer Mynydd. Go to a small gate ahead on the right, then along the field edge to a stile. Follow the waymarked path across open ground – *enjoying extensive coastal views* – through an old gateway, past old stiles and on to a stile. Follow the path through small trees, gorse and heather down to a ladder-stile. Follow the fence down past gorse and along the field edge to a ladder-stile and along the next field.

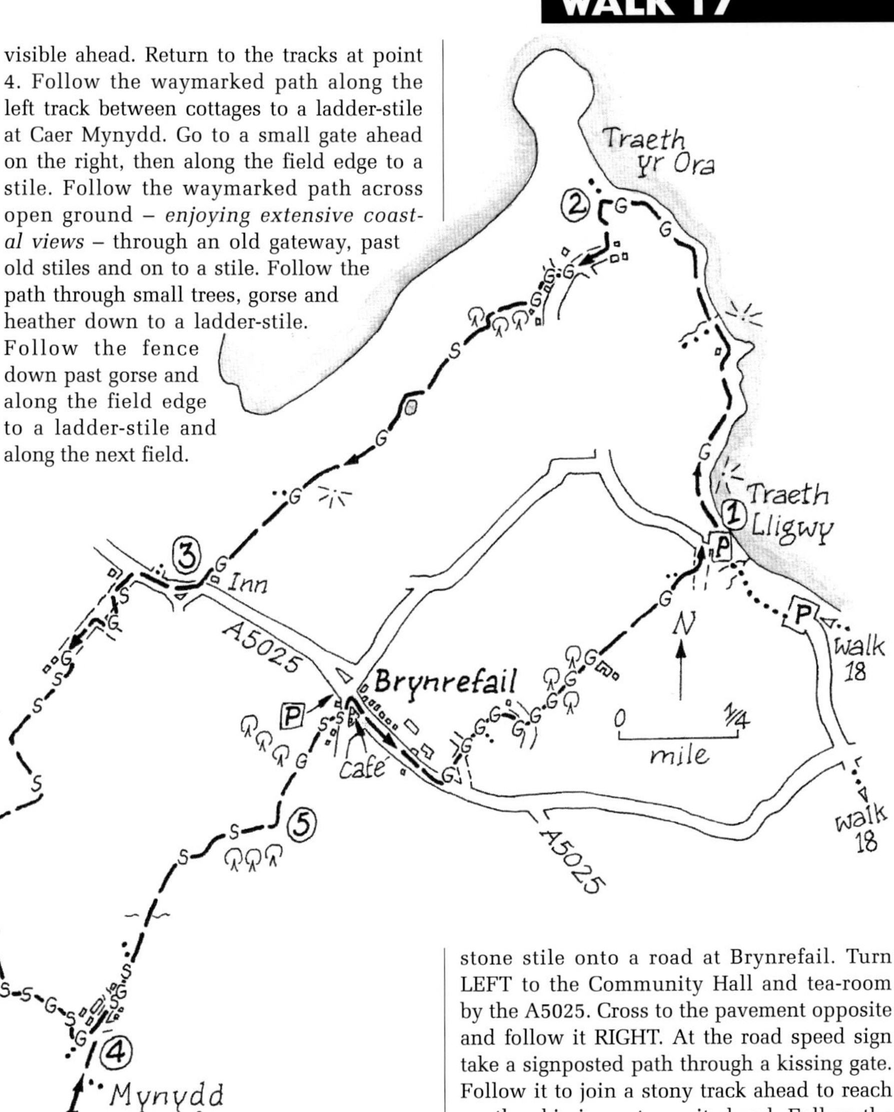

5 At a waymark post by a tree turn LEFT. Go past another, descend and continue along the field edge past a waymarked wood boundary corner, then a post down to a kissing gate. Follow the boundary on your right to a stone stile by a cottage and on to a gated stone stile onto a road at Brynrefail. Turn LEFT to the Community Hall and tea-room by the A5025. Cross to the pavement opposite and follow it RIGHT. At the road speed sign take a signposted path through a kissing gate. Follow it to join a stony track ahead to reach another kissing gate on its bend. Follow the path ahead to a kissing gate, then to another in the boundary. Follow the large hedge boundary to a kissing gate at the entrance to Siop y Rhon. Go to gates opposite and follow the path to a kissing gate, then through trees to another and on to a further kissing gate by a farm building. Follow the path to a kissing gate and through trees, then turn LEFT along a stony track to reach the nearby car park. *The other beach car park shown, accessed by the CP, has a seasonal café.*

WALK 18

TRAETH LLIGWY & DIN LLIGWY

DESCRIPTION A contrasting 4¼ mile walk full of interest, including two impressive ancient monuments. The route first follows the cliff top Coastal Path (CP) past the Seawatch Centre and a memorial to the sinking of the Royal Charter in Porth Helaeth in 1859 to Traeth Lligwy car park, with toilets and seasonal cafe. It then returns via Din Lligwy and a Neolithic burial chamber. At Din Lligwy are the substantial remains of a Romano British settlement of stone buildings. This defended settlement containing round and rectangular huts of various dates, and a workshop, was mainly occupied during 4thC AD. Allow about 2½ hours.

START Moelfre car park [SH 512862].

DIRECTIONS On entering Moelfre on the A5108, turn left to a car park with toilets on the left adjoining Ffordd Lligwy. Another car park is nearby.

Moelfre, once associated with a thriving herring industry, is perhaps best known for the sterling work of its lifeboat and crews. Since 1830 until the present day they have saved hundreds of shipwrecked mariners. Sadly it could not prevent the loss of over 400 lives and £300, 000 of gold when the Royal Charter clipper on route from Melbourne to Liverpool was hit by a hurricane. It was seen as a national disaster attracting many visitors, including Charles Dickens.

1 Take the path leading from the toilets to the road. Cross to the left of the bus shelter opposite to take a pathway between houses to join the road by Ann's Pantry. Turn LEFT down the road, then go across the beach car park and follow a path down to rejoin the road. Follow it past the small pebbly beach up to the bend. Here take the signposted Coastal Path round past houses then the original lifeboat station and Seawatch Centre – *containing interesting displays, relics from the Royal Charter and other local wrecks, as well as a lifeboat and RNLI gift shop.* Continue along the surfaced path past the current lifeboat station, then a rough path above the pebbly shore and on to a stone memorial seat to the rescue of the crew of the Hindlea in 1959 from this headland. Follow the cliff-top path past a modern sculpture then above Porth Helaeth. After a kissing gate the CP continues between hedges to another kissing gate, then across the edge of a caravan park to an information board on The Royal Charter by a kissing gate. Soon the CP rises to a stone stile giving access to the Royal Charter monument. Afterwards continue with the cliff-top path to a good viewpoint across Porth Forllwyd. *Just off the coast on the small rock of Ynys Dulas is a distinctive small tower, which was built in 1824 as a refuge for shipwrecked sailors, stocked with food and water.* After a kissing gate by a house go along its access track. At the entrance to a large house turn RIGHT to another kissing gate. *Nearby is a small sandy beach and the remains of a small stone jetty.* Go along the field edge to another kissing gate at a viewpoint overlooking Lligwy Bay and on along the cliffs to reach Traeth Lligwy car park.

2 From the car park follow the road past dwellings and Dafarn Rhos Caravan & Camping site. At crossroads go up the road ahead past Tyn-Lon. Shortly, go through a kissing gate on the right signposted to Din Lligwy. *Nearby is the ruin of a 12thC Chapel of Ease.* Follow the waymarked path along field edges to kissing gates and up through the trees to visit Din Lligwy. Afterwards, return to continue along the road – *enjoying extensive views east along the coast to the Great Orme and Snowdonia mountains.* Shortly a kissing gate on the right gives access to Lligwy Neolithic burial chamber. *Built before 3000 BC, it contained the remains of 30 men, women and children. Continue along the road.* Later, just before the road begins to rise through trees, take a signposted path through a kissing gate on the left. Go along the tree-lined field edge to another kissing gate, then an enclosed path past woodland to a further kissing gate.

Go up the field to a small gate and continue along the next field, soon bending left to a kissing gate. Just beyond turn RIGHT past outbuildings of a nearby house, then follow its access road to a school. At the road beyond, follow it RIGHT back to the start.

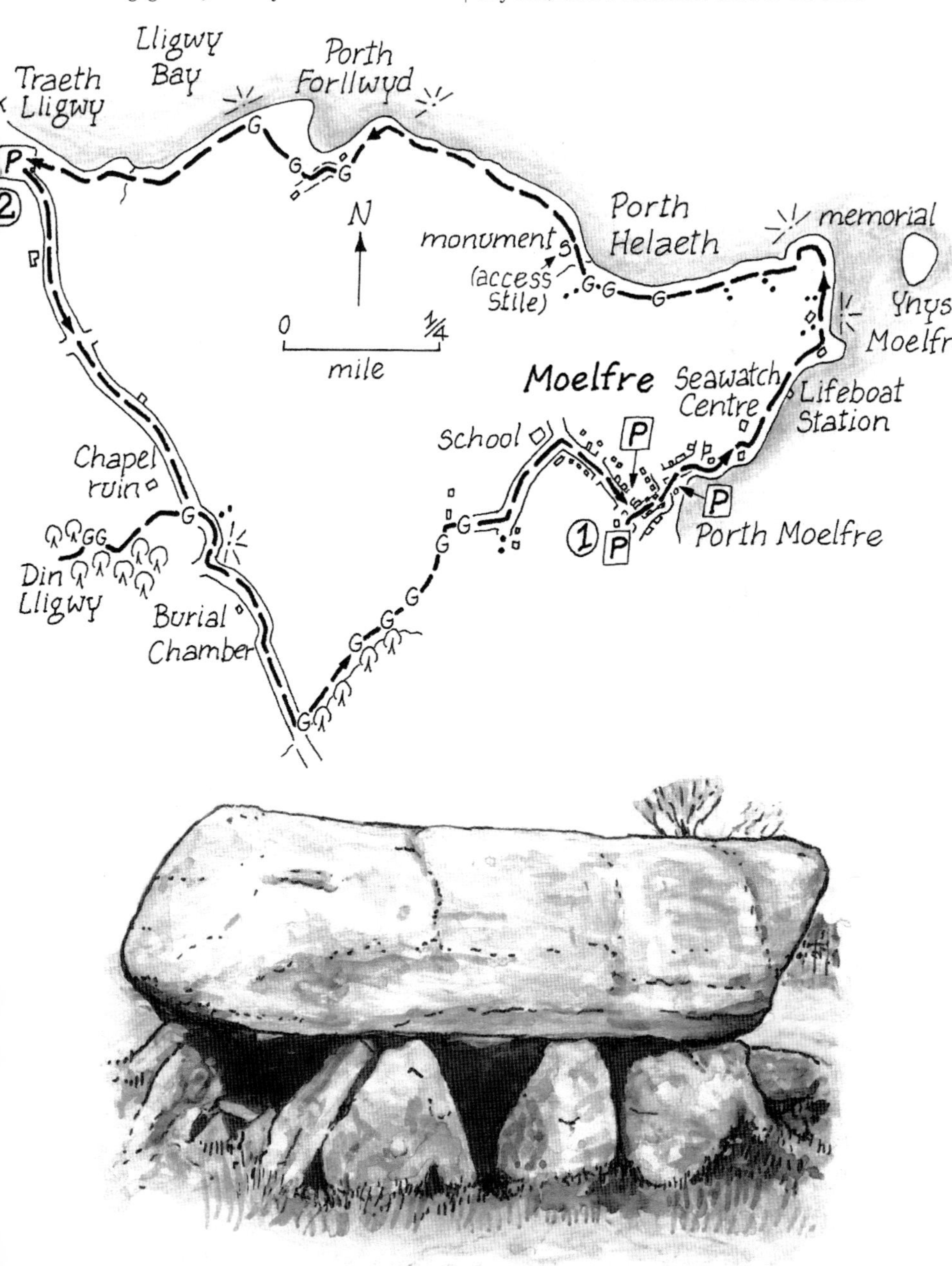

Neolithic burial chamber

WALK 19

TRAETH COCH

DESCRIPTION A varied 5½ mile walk (**A**) from Pentraeth to Traeth Coch (Red Wharf Bay). The walk follows an attractive route down to the beach car park at Traeth Coch, then incorporates the beach (avoid at high tide) and inland woodland sections of the Coastal Path (CP), before returning to Pentraeth. Allow about 3 hours. For a 3 mile walk (**B**) just combining both Coastal Path sections start from Traeth Coch car park and follow instructions from point 2.
START Car park, Pentraeth [SH 524785] or Traeth Coch car park [SH535799].
DIRECTIONS Driving north on the A5025 through Pentraeth the car park is on the right. For the Traeth Coch car park see Walk 20.

__Traeth Coch__ (Red Wharf Bay) is a beautiful large bay with an extensive area of sand at low tide. It was once a safe anchorage for ships, and used for coastal trading and the shipping of local quarried limestone. Nearby Pentraeth, with its 12thC church, is an ancient village standing on the crossroads of old routes.

1 From information boards at Pentraeth car park entrance go down Brick Street and over the river. After it becomes Chapel Bank, just after Drws-y-Nant, go through a kissing gate on the right by a cattle-grid and along an access track. Just beyond a cattle grid follow the signposted path ahead along the edge of two fields, then an enclosed path to Bay View Farm. Follow its access track down and on past Rose Cottage to Pen y Lon at the edge of Traeth Coch. Follow the signposted Coastal Path RIGHT along the wide track, then road, crossing a bridge over the river to a road junction. Turn LEFT to the beach car park.

2 Take the signposted Coastal Path along the edge of Traeth Coch, later on a sandy track. After 1 mile at a CP fingerpost just beyond chalet Ger-y-Mor turn RIGHT through trees on the signposted CP inland route to the nearby hidden road end.

3 Follow the signposted CP along Coch-y-Mieri's access track, shortly leaving it to pass behind the house. At a waymarked path junction, descend the ladder-stile and follow the CP through three kissing gates then behind a house. After another kissing gate the path rises to a waymarked path junction. Take the CP right fork down to a track. Follow it LEFT down to join another access track. Follow it to a signposted path junction by two houses. Bear RIGHT with the CP along the track. At its end either continue by road or turn RIGHT to follow a signposted path along the road down to Glan Morfa and the shore beyond for a return to the beach car park. For **Walk A** then return to Pentraeth by road or your outward route.

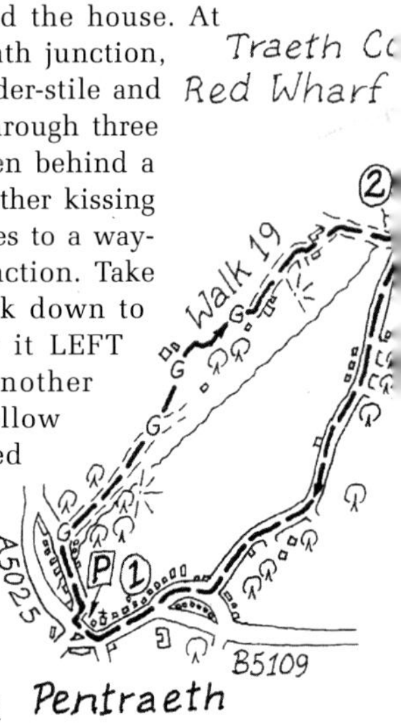

WALK 20

COED PENTRAETH

DESCRIPTION An undulating 7¼ mile (**A**) or 6 mile (**B**) of great variety exploring the edge of Traeth Coch (Red Wharf Bay). The route passes through Pentraeth Forest, a home for the endangered Red squirrel, then crosses attractive countryside to the eastern end of Traeth Coch returning by either inland or shoreline sections of the Coastal Path (CP). Allow about 4½ hours.
START Beach car park, Traeth Coch [SH 535799].
DIRECTIONS In Pentraeth take the B5109 (Beaumaris) past the Panton Arms. Take the first road on the left, then the next left, signposted to the beach, to the car park at its end.

1 Return along the road then follow the signposted Coastal Path LEFT along the no through road past dwellings and up to where it bends left towards Glan Morfa. Follow the CP along the joining track to two houses. Here turn RIGHT on another signposted path up a track. On its bend where it splits into three, go up the narrow track directly ahead to a small gate on the left. Go up the stony track and through a small gate on the left opposite an old barn. The path rises through trees past a waymarked side path to a kissing gate into Coed Pentraeth, then continues up to a forestry track. Follow it LEFT, then as it begins to bend left bear RIGHT to a nearby waymarked path junction at a barrier. Take the path ahead through the forest on a gentle descent, later on a more discernible old track. About 25 yards before it bends left take a waymarked path on the right (easy to miss). Follow it past two white-topped posts, then down to a boardwalked section at a waymarked path junction by a footbridge over a stream. Turn LEFT over a side stream and along the wood edge by the stream to a small gate. Go along the right-hand field edge to continue beside the stream, then fence, to a stiled/gated footbridge over the stream.

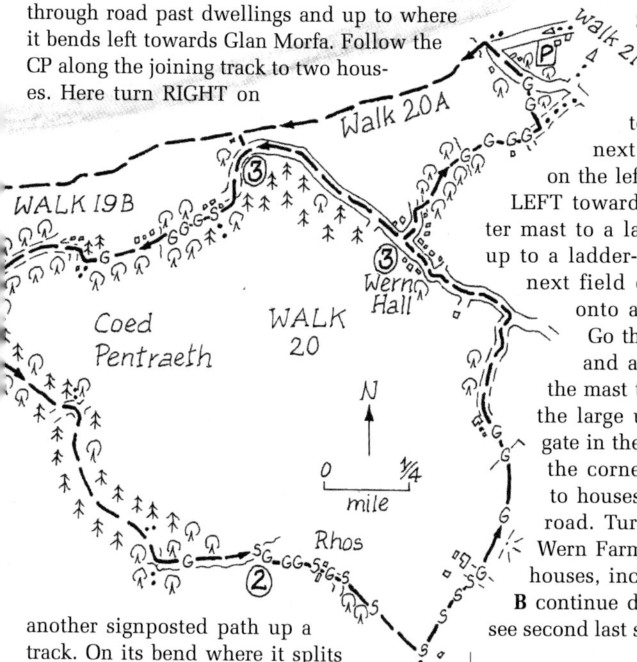

2 Keep ahead, soon at a waymark post bearing LEFT to another post, small gate and another beyond. Follow the waymarked path beside the fence then between boundaries up to Rhos. Go through the old farm to a gate and along its old green access track to a ladder-stile/gate on its bend. Go along the wooded field edge to a ladder-stile and along the next field to cross a ladder-stile on the left in the narrow corner. Angle LEFT towards the distant large transmitter mast to a ladder-stile. Follow the fence up to a ladder-stile in it then go along the next field edge to another ladder-stile onto a nearby farm's access track. Go through a kissing gate opposite and across the large field towards the mast to a gate. Go half-LEFT across the large undulating field to a kissing gate in the boundary on your left before the corner. Follow the enclosed path to houses, then their access track to a road. Turn LEFT down the road past Wern Farm Estate, then other attractive houses, including Wern Hall. (For **Walk B** continue down the road to its end then see second last sentence below.)

3 For **Walk A** take a signposted path along a private road on the right by the entrance to Gwynaeteth, then access track down past houses. At the last take a signposted path leading right to a footbridge over a stream. Follow the undulating path through the wood past a waymarked side path to a kissing gate. The path continues across more open ground then through trees and two further kissing gates. Follow the enclosed path to another kissing gate then continue down a track. Just before it enters trees turn LEFT down another track, through gates and on to a road. Follow it LEFT. Just beyond Glan Helen take the signposted path ahead through trees to a crossroad of paths on the shore edge. Turn LEFT and follow the waymarked CP across a footbridge over the river, along the edge of low dunes, then a part boardwalked section. It continues along the sea wall and on past bullrushes to a CP fingerpost. For the inland route turn LEFT through trees to the nearby hidden road end. Follow instructions in paragraph 3 of Walk 19 back to the beach car park. Alternatively if tidal conditions permit follow the CP along the shoreline.

WALK 21

BWRDD ARTHUR

DESCRIPTION A 4½ mile meandering and undulating walk to Bwrdd Athur hillfort (538 feet/164 metres), an Open Access area, offering panoramic views, returning on the Coastal Path (CP). Allow about 3 hours.
START Traeth Coch (east) beach car park [SH 568806].
DIRECTIONS The car park with toilets and seasonal cafe is reached by a steep minor road from the northern end of Llanddona.

Bwrdd Arthur (Arthur's Table), also known as Din Sylwy, is a small limestone hill containing the remains of a hillfort built in the Iron Age and occupied during the later Roman period. Quarries on the nearby cliffs provided limestone for the Menai Suspension Bridge.

1 Return along the road, soon bending inland. Later take a signposted path along a track past a cottage to a kissing gate at its end. Follow the field path through further kissing gates to a track by a house. Turn RIGHT up a hedge/tree-lined path to a house. Go past its right-hand side and up to a kissing gate by an old ruin. Just beyond go up the path's left fork to a waymarked junction. Turn LEFT up the path to a kissing gate, then go up the road. At the T-junction turn LEFT down the road. On the bend take the signposted bridleway through the entrance to Ysgubor Penrallt, then go down the left fork. Shortly the tree-lined bridleway narrows, then does a U -turn and heads north to eventually emerge at the entrance to Hafod Wen. Go down its access track.

2 Just before Tros yr Afon turn RIGHT up steps and follow a path up to join an access track which rises to a road. Go up the road and past a transmitter mast. At the junction turn LEFT then cross a stile beneath Bwrdd Arthur. Follow a path beside the fence and up onto the hillfort for great views from its trig point and eastern ramparts. Return to the stile. Now follow a path along Bwrdd Arthur's lower western slopes. Shortly turn sharp left down a farm track to a kissing gate. (If before you reach the track the path is closed, as is being proposed, a short new link path will take you left to the kissing gate.) Follow a path west along the field edge to another kissing gate, and down to a kissing gate into National Trust owned Bryn Offa, then down the gorse-covered hillside to a farm track.

3 Go across the track and follow the signposted Coastal Path down through scrub, then the right-hand edge of a field to a gap and a kissing gate in the bottom corner. The CP continues through more scrub to a kissing gate, then turns RIGHT down an access track to a gate just before Godreddi Mawr. Follow the CP to a kissing gate and down a field to another. Go along the low cliffs to a kissing gate, then the edge of the rocky shore to a footbridge over a stream. Continue along the beach or adjoining road to the start.

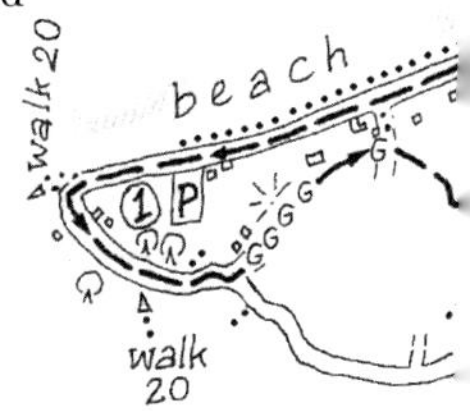

WALK 22

FEDW FAWR

DESCRIPTION A 6¾ mile walk **(A)** featuring the cliffs of National Trust owned Fedw Fawr, ancient churches and Bwrdd Arthur Iron Age hillfort offering panoramic views. Allow about 4 hours. The route includes a 4½ mile walk **(B)** just to Fedw Fawr and a 2½ mile walk **(C)** to Mariandyrys Nature Reserve, an area of limestone owned by North Wales Wildlife Trust.
START Llangoed car park [SH 610796].
DIRECTIONS See Walk 23.

1 Go across the bridge and up the road ahead. Soon, take a signposted path along a track on the left past the former village pub and on past other dwellings to a kissing gate. Turn RIGHT up the field edge to a road. Follow it LEFT, shortly rising to a former Victorian school and continuing to

St Cawrdaf's church. *Largely rebuilt in 1881, its north transept dating from 1612 survives from an earlier church. It was dedicated to Cawrdaf, an ancient Welsh chief.* Turn LEFT on a signposted path by the churchyard wall and up a field to a road by a cottage. Go along the narrow road past dwellings to a dip by cottages just before a junction. (For **Walk C** go through a kissing gate and follow the path to another road at point 5. Go up the road to a stile giving access to an information board and Mariandyrys Nature Reserve. Follow the path up onto the ridge beyond a cottage for extensive views, then return to point 5.)

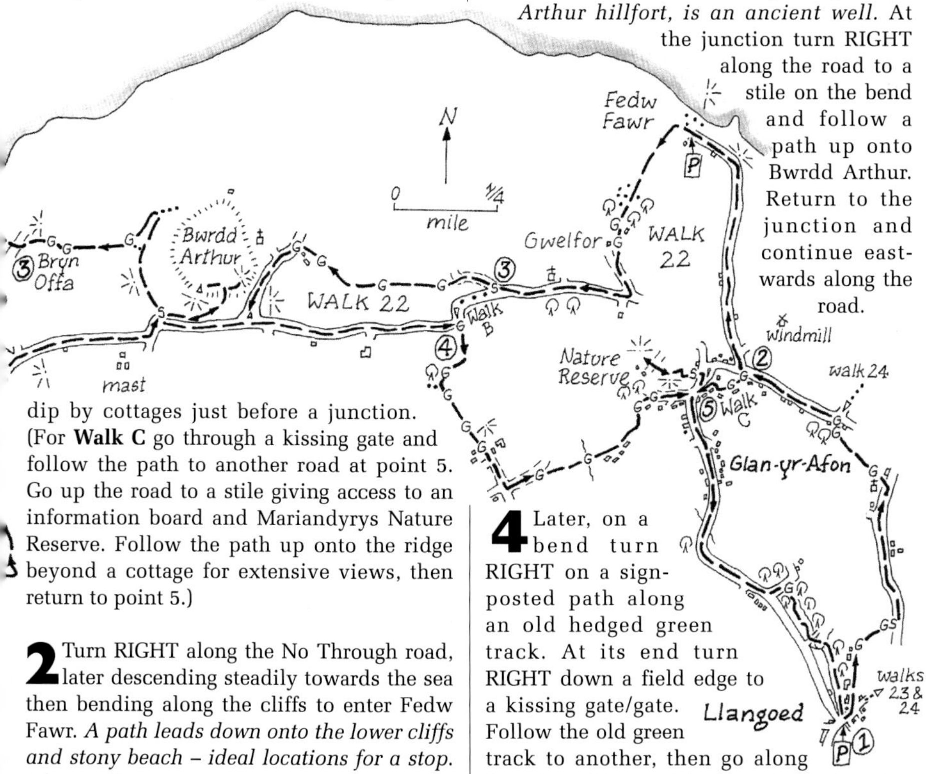

2 Turn RIGHT along the No Through road, later descending steadily towards the sea then bending along the cliffs to enter Fedw Fawr. *A path leads down onto the lower cliffs and stony beach – ideal locations for a stop.* Afterwards continue up the old narrow green track, soon bending left on a wide path up the part gorse/heather-covered hillside. Near the top pass side paths, then take the path's left fork past a small water but. Follow the narrowing path through trees to a small gate, leaving Fedw Fawr. The path continues to a kissing gate by Gwelfor cottage, goes along a field edge, then follows its access track to a road. Follow it RIGHT past Llanfihangel Methodist Sunday School built in 1887.

3 Shortly take the signposted Coastal Path along Fargen Wen's access track. (For **Walk B** continue along the road to point 4.) On the bend follow the waymarked path down through gorse to a ladder-stile, and along the edge of two large fields – *with Bwrdd Arthur ahead* – then past Ty Mawr to a road/track. Follow the road LEFT past the entrance to Llanfihangel Din Sylwy church. *Near the simple 15thC church, renovated in 1855, standing below the ramparts of Bwrdd Arthur hillfort, is an ancient well.* At the junction turn RIGHT along the road to a stile on the bend and follow a path up onto Bwrdd Arthur. Return to the junction and continue eastwards along the road.

4 Later, on a bend turn RIGHT on a signposted path along an old hedged green track. At its end turn RIGHT down a field edge to a kissing gate/gate. Follow the old green track to another, then go along the edge of two fields down to Penhwnllys Plas. Follow a short enclosed path to join its access track. Follow it to the bend of a road. Turn LEFT along a hedge-lined green track to a kissing gate on the right then turn LEFT along the field edge to a gate. Follow the field edge past a farm round to a gate in the corner. Follow the enclosed path past a house, then turn RIGHT down an access track to a road. Turn RIGHT.

5 Follow the road down through Glan-yr-Afon. Later at the Llangoed road sign turn LEFT along a lane to a kissing gate on the right. Now follow the path through the woodland Local Nature Reserve to Llangoed.

WALK 23

PENMON PRIORY

DESCRIPTION A 4½ mile walk **(A)** featuring Castell Aberlleiniog, a Motte and Bailey castle, a Holy Well and a number of interesting buildings at the site of Penmon Priory (see below). Allow about 2½ hours. A shorter 1½ mile walk **(B)** to Castell Aberlleiniog is included.

START Llangoed car park [SH 610796].

DIRECTIONS From Beaumaris take the B5109 to Llangoed. Go through the village to find a car park on the right.

*In the **6thC** St Seiriol founded a monastery at Penmon. Its church was rebuilt in stone in the 12thC and remains in use today. In the early 13thC the site became an Augustinian Priory, until its dissolution in 1537. Under the subsequent ownership of the Bulkeley family of Beaumaris, the prior's dwellings were converted into an attractive residence and in the 18thC land used as an extensive walled deer park. Available to visit are the priory ruins, the 12C church, St Siriol's original Holy Well, and an early 17thC Dovecot.*

1 From the car park entrance turn RIGHT across the bridge and up the road ahead out of the village. Shortly turn RIGHT along a side road past Haulfre. After bends go through a kissing gate on the right and follow the enclosed path signposted to the castle. After a section of boardwalk take the path's left fork up to a path junction. Follow the path ahead waymarked 'entrance' round the back of the castle to information boards at its stepped entrance. *Originally built in the late 11thC, the existing stone walls and towers date from the 17thC when it was used in the Civil War. The Home Guard occupied it in World War II.* After visiting its interior continue along the stony path, over a footbridge, past a side path on the right and on down through trees. At a path junction follow the raised wooden path ahead, bending sharply down to a wide stony path. Follow it through trees to cross a bridge over the river to a signposted path T-junction. (For **Walk B** turn right and follow the riverside woodland path, then lane back to the start.)

2 Turn LEFT (traeth/beach) to gates, then follow the wide stony path, initially through woodland, to a kissing gate. Go along the road, soon joined by the Coastal Path, to pass the entrance to a shoreline car park. Just beyond Lleiniog cottages follow a section of old road angling right to a house entrance, then the Coastal Path through trees and down to the stony beach. Go along its edge past an old boathouse and on to rejoin the road - *enjoying great views along the Menai Strait and across to Snowdonia.* Continue along the road – *later with a view across Porth Penmon to shoreline limekilns. Penmon 'marble' (limestone) was quarried locally until the early 20thC and taken down inclined planes to the old quay you pass. It was used for Penmon Priory, at Beaumaris and Penrhyn Castles, for both bridges across the Menai Strait and for many prestigious buildings.* Eventually you reach Penmon Priory and church.

3 After visiting the nearby Dovecot and Holy Well return along the road, then just past the old Priory take a path angling RIGHT to steps and a small iron gate, then turn LEFT near the wall. At a building go half-RIGHT up a green track, then along a field edge past old workings. At the top end of a line of limestone ignore a path leading to a higher limestone ridge, but contour across the field towards distant chimneys to a small iron gate in the wall ahead. Turn LEFT down the road. At a junction turn RIGHT past Bryn Mawr farm. On the bend go through a kissing gate on the left. After a small gate follow the fence down to a kissing gate onto a road. Follow it RIGHT to join your outward route.

WALK 24

PENMON POINT

DESCRIPTION A 6½ mile walk following Walk 23 to Penmon Priory, then continuing to Penmon Point, opposite Puffin Island, with its interesting café (www.pilothousecafe.com). It returns on a section of the Coastal Path (CP), then via St. Cawrdaf's church. Allow about 4 hours.

START As Walk 23..

***Penmon Point** has played an important role in the protection of shipping, following the loss nearby of 130 people on the steamer Rothsay Castle in 1831. A lifeboat station*

(1832–1915) was involved in 50 rescues and the saving of 116 lives. A Coastguard rescue station operates here today. Standing in the narrow sound is a lighthouse beacon built in 1838 to keep ships away from submerged rocks. It became automated in 1922. Nearby Puffin Island contains the ruins of a monastic settlement first established in the 6thC by St. Seiriol and a former 19thC telegraph station. In the 1890s rats got onto the island and decimated the many Puffins and other seabirds, but in 1998 efforts began to kill the rats to enable birds to return.

1-2 Follow instructions in paragraphs 1-2 of Walk 23 to Penmon Priory.

3 From the Dovecot continue up the road, later descending past Penmon Coastguard rescue station and Pilot House café to Penmon Point by former Trinity House pilot houses. Return up the road then at the café take the signposted Coastal Path angling off on the right up and across an area of bracken and scrub to a kissing gate and on to a road. Turn RIGHT to a nearby kissing gate and go along the field edge to another kissing gate. Now follow the gated path alongside the large wall enclosing the former Deer Park up to a road by a cottage. Follow it past other dwellings, later passing a junction, then follow the CP RIGHT along an access track past Tyn y Coed to a kissing gate just before two other dwellings.

4 Follow the kissing gated CP to an access track by a cottage. The CP continues through further kissing gates, passes a cottage and goes up its access track. Soon it turns RIGHT and continues via gates to a stony access track by houses. Follow it RIGHT to a road. Go through a kissing gate opposite and follow the enclosed CP down to a stone stile, then LEFT along a track down to a road. Go through a kissing gate opposite by a cottage and another below. Follow the path down the field to the road by St Cawrdaf's church. *Largely rebuilt in 1881, its north transept dating from 1612 survives from an earlier church. It was dedicated to Cawrdaf, an ancient Welsh chief.* Continue along the road, past the old Victorian school and down past two houses. Later, take a signposted path on the right into a field. Follow the boundary down to a kissing gate in it. Go past a cottage and along its access track to the road in Llangoed near the start.

WALK 25

LLANIDAN

DESCRIPTION A 3¾ mile walk combining shoreline (restricted at high tide) and inland sections of the Coastal Path and featuring historic houses. Allow about 2½ hours.
START Brynsiencyn car park [SH 485671].
DIRECTIONS The car park is at the eastern end of the village opposite Y Groeslon.

***Brynsiencyn** developed during the late 18th/19thC from a farming community to one linked with slate quarrying at Dinorwic, Llanberis on the mainland. Men would cross by ferry and spend the week at basic barracks.*

1 From the car park turn RIGHT down the road, later being joined by the Coastal Path at the entrance to Llan Idan farm, to the large wall enclosing 17thC Plas Llanidan – *once the home of Thomas Williams, the 'Copper King' (1737–1802) who made his fortunes from Anglesey copper mines. Also here, but now privately owned, is 15thC Llanidan church, dedicated to St Aidan, a 7thC bishop.* Here the road and Coastal Path split. Take its right fork beside the boundary wall, then continue along a tree-line stony track – *enjoying a view across the Menai Strait to the the mountains of Snowdonia* – shortly bending right then descending to the tree-lined edge of the Strait. Follow the Coastal Path down a track to the shore, then along the walled edge of the pebbly beach past a wooden boathouse, later curving round to an old stone jetty after ½ mile.

2 Go through a nearby kissing gate, then follow the Coastal Path inland to the bend of a road. Follow the road ahead to go past outbuildings at Plas Porthamel. Follow the signposted Coastal Path LEFT along a track, past woodland, later joining an access lane and passing houses. At a T-junction turn LEFT along the road, soon joining your outward route at Llanidan to return to Brynsiencyn.

WALK 26

MENAI STRAIT

DESCRIPTION A 4¼ mile walk featuring a section of Coastal Path (CP) near the Menai Strait, and the opportunity to visit Anglesey Sea Zoo, Wales' largest marine aquarium with café, and Halen Mon (Anglesey Sea Salt). Allow about 2½ hours.
START As Walk 25.

***The Menai Strait** is a 15 mile long narrow channel dividing Anglesey from the mainland. It is subject to unusual and rapid tidal flows, which for centuries has made it hazardous to shipping. Ferries operated across the Strait from 1296 until 1954. It is crossed by two innovative and historic 19thC bridges: the Menai Suspension Bridge and the Britannia Bridge. Its various habitats support many species and it is a Special Area of Conservation. It has an important mussel and oyster fishery.*

1 From the car park turn RIGHT down the road to the entrance to Llan Idan farm. Take the Coastal Path opposite across the field to a kissing gate in the far right hand corner. Follow the waymarked path through the wood edge to a kissing gate. The kissing gated CP now continues through several fields – *enjoying views of the Menai Strait and the mountains of Snowdonia beyond* – then briefly along the pebbly shore to a road. Continue along the shoreline road passing the entrances to Halen Mon and adjoining Anglesey Sea Zoo, and a short cut path. At the junction – *with a view across to Caernarfon Castle* – turn RIGHT up the road.

2 Shortly take a signposted path on the right, opposite an access track to nearby dwellings. Go across two fields, then in the next follow the fence round to a small gate in it. Cross a ladder-stile ahead into the Sea Zoo. Bear RIGHT past its entrance, then along its driveway past the children's play area. At its corner turn LEFT across a bridge over a stream into Halen Mon. Turn LEFT along the edge of its car park to a kissing gate and a nearby gate. Go up the field to the bend of a road at the entrance to Tai Cochion. Follow it ahead past award-winning home bakery Popty'r Bryn at Cefn Arthen. Later at a junction turn LEFT along the side road past dwellings to a kissing gate on the right. Follow the gated path through several small fields, past a house and on through two further fields to an access lane by a house. Turn RIGHT along the nearby road into Brynsiencyn, continuing along the main road to the start.

WALK 27

CAER LEB

DESCRIPTION A 2¼ mile walk along quiet lanes and field paths to visit Caer Leb, an Iron Age defended settlement with double banks and ditches, used until the Roman period, now managed by Cadw. Allow about 1½ hours.
START As Walk 25.

1 Follow the A4080 (Newborough) through the village past the shop. When it bends right go along Lon Uchaf, soon leaving the village. Follow the road to a T-junction. Turn RIGHT then LEFT at the next nearby junction. At another junction bend right to the A4080. Go along the road opposite past Brynderwydd. Later cross a ladder-stile on the right. Go along the long field edge to another ladder-stile, then along the next past the distinctive earthworks of Caer Leb in the adjoining field to a road. Turn RIGHT. A nearby gate gives access to view the monument. Afterwards continue up the road to the A4080. Turn LEFT along the pavement, soon bending up to the village. At the entrance to Plas Siencyn opposite Ty'n Cwrt estate turn LEFT on a signposted path along an access track past houses. After Cae'r Pant go through a kissing gate on the right. Go up the edge of three fields to a stile by houses. At an access track beyond turn RIGHT then LEFT between buildings to the main road. Follow it to the start.

WALK 28
YNYS LLANDDWYN (1)

DESCRIPTION A 4½ mile (**A**) or 3¾ mile (**B**) walk featuring attractive forest, an award winning beach, panoramic views and a visit to the historic romantic Llanddwyn island, accessible except at high tide (check tide tables). Allow about 3 hours.
START Newborough Forest car park [SH 406635].
DIRECTIONS From Newborough follow a minor road signposted to the beach, later through the forest (toll payable), to the large car park.

Llanddwyn *is named after St Dwynwen, patron saint of Welsh lovers, who allegedly lived here in the 5thC, and whose legend attracted pilgrims here in later centuries. Today this small beautiful island, part of a National Nature Reserve, is a fascinating place to visit, with superb views. It contains the ruins of a 16thC church dedicated to St Dwynwen and two large crosses. At its tip are an early 19thC stone beacon tower, now with a modern light, and a windmill shaped lighthouse built in 1845, which was deactivated in 1975. Nearby are cottages (now containing an exhibition) built in the mid-19thC for pilots who guided ships through the Menai Strait. Outside is a cannon used to call the crew of a lifeboat based here from 1840 until 1903. In 2004 the island was used as a film location for the romantic thriller 'Half Light', starring Demi Moore..*

1 From the entrance follow the Coastal Path along a road then track westwards through the forest to an informal beach car park. Follow the beach round to an information board and onto Ynys Llanddwyn. Follow the waymarked Ynys Llanddwyn path clockwise round the island. Afterwards return along the beach past the first car park. (For **Walk B** later go through the dunes to the main car park.) For **Walk A** continue east along the beach then at the forest corner follow a path up through the dunes. Shortly, follow the Coastal Path LEFT through trees and along a track back to the start.

WALK 29
LLYS RHOSYR

DESCRIPTION A 2¾ mile walk to the part excavated site of a 13thC Royal Court of the Welsh Princes discovered in 1992, followed by a short section of Newborough Forest. Allow about 2 hours.
START Llyn Rhos Ddu car park [SH 427648].
DIRECTIONS Entering Newborough from the east, at a roundabout follow the no through road ahead to the car park. (A path leads to a hide overlooking nearby Llyn Rhos Ddu.)

1 From the National Nature Reserve information board follow the signposted Coastal Path west to a signposted crossroad of paths by another information board. Turn RIGHT (signposted to Newborough) along a track then up a lane past dwellings. At a junction first go to the bend ahead to visit Llys Rhosyr then return to continue along the road (beach) to a kissing gate on the right opposite Tirmawr. Follow the field path to a kissing gate into Newborough Forest, then the stony path ahead to where it splits at post 30.

2 Take the left fork, a narrow green track, to a road beyond a cottage. Follow it RIGHT. Shortly, at a no parking sign, turn LEFT past a barrier and follow the wide waymarked red trail through the forest. At its edge turn LEFT on the waymarked Coastal Path/Heritage Walk, shortly on an access track, to join your outward route.

WALK 30
NEWBOROUGH WARREN

DESCRIPTION A 3½ mile waymarked walk through one of the largest sand dune landscapes in Europe and a National Nature Reserve to a stunning viewpoint. Allow about 2½ hours.
START As Walk 29.

1 From the National Nature Reserve information board follow the signposted Coastal Path to a crossroad of paths by another information board. Go through the smaller of two gates and follow the path signposted to Abermenai across the sand dunes, guided by regular small waymark posts, to eventually reach a gate and a bench at the edge of the dunes offering a superb panorama of mountains. Follow a path below LEFT along the saltmarsh edge to another bench. Enter the dunes, then from a nearby gate follow the waymarked path back across the Warren to a road by a small car park. Follow it to the junction and back to the start.

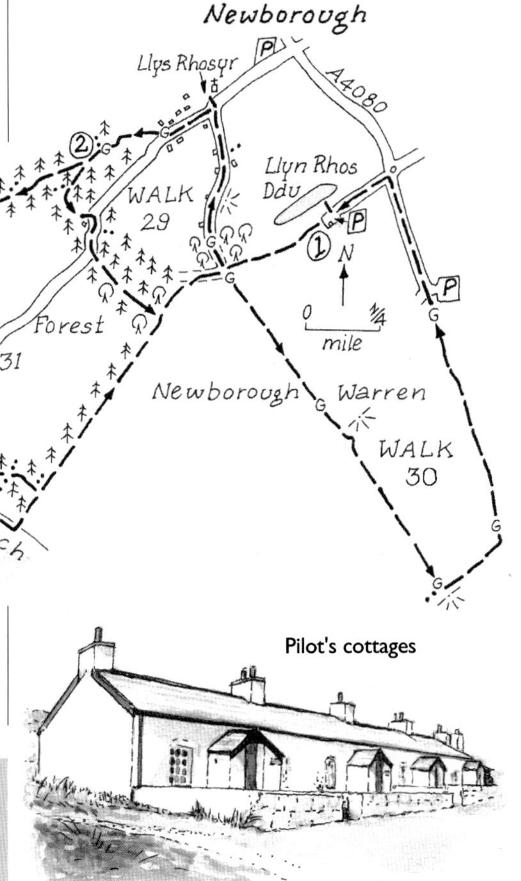

Pilot's cottages

WALK 31
YNYS LLANDDWYN (2)

DESCRIPTION A 7¾ mile walk via Llys Rhosyr and Newborough Forest to Llanddwyn island (See Walk 28), accessible except at high tide, returning along the beach [a] or Coastal Path [b], then continuing with the CP past Newborough Warren. Allow about 4½ hours.
START As Walk 29.

1 Follow instructions in paragraph 1 of Walk 29.

2 Take the waymarked white trail right fork to a wide stony track, then continue ahead along a narrow green track (a waymarked blue Horse Trail in reverse) down to a stony track. Follow it ahead down to a wider track beyond a barrier. Follow the Coastal Path/track ahead to an informal car park overlooking Llanddwyn beach. Follow the beach round to Ynys Llanddwyn, then a waymarked path clockwise round the island. Afterwards return along the beach. (For route [**b**] from the informal car park follow the Coastal Path along the forestry track to the main car park, round its edge onto the dunes, then east along a track and through trees to the forest edge.) For route [**a**] continue east along the beach. At the forest corner turn up through the dunes, then along the forest edge. Both routes then follow the Coastal Path along the forest edge past the dunes of Newborough Warren, then an access track to reach your outward route.

WALK 32

NEWBOROUGH FOREST

DESCRIPTION A 7¼ mile walk around attractive Newborough Forest, using the Coastal Path and various waymarked recreational trails. It includes visits to lovely Penrhos and Llanddwyn beaches to view historic romantic Ynys Llanddwyn (See Walk 28), accessible except at high tide. Allow about 4½ hours. If tidal conditions are suitable (check tide tables) an additional 1¾ miles walk around Llanddwyn island can be included.

START Pen Cob Newborough National Nature Reserve car park [SH 411671] or Llyn Parc Mawr car park [SH 414671].

DIRECTIONS Pen Cob car park lies on the western side of the A4080, 1 mile south of Malltraeth. Llyn Parc Mawr car park lies on the eastern side.

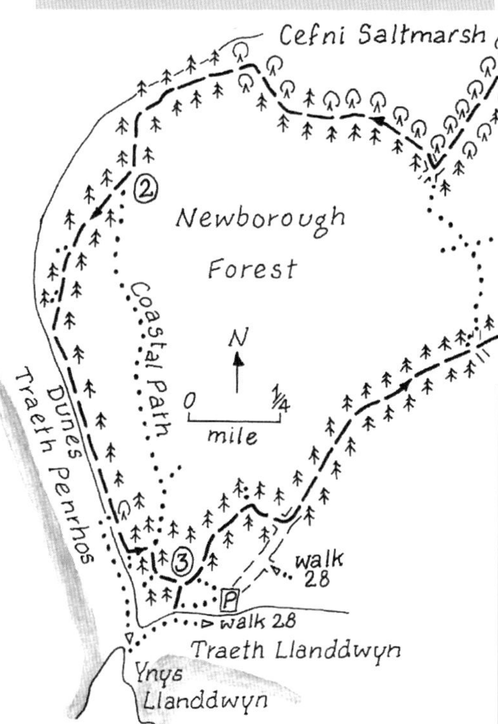

Newborough Forest *was planted with Corsican Pine trees between 1947 and 1965 for timber and to protect Newborough from the advance of wind-blown sand. It is an important habitat for wildlife and one of the UK's most important sites for the threatened red squirrel. It is also a popular recreational area.*

1 From Pen Cob car park follow the signposted Coastal Path (CP) and blue/black Horse Trails (HT) along the forest edge near the road. Opposite the Llyn Parc Mawr car park entrance the trails continue southwards along a wide stony track through Newborough Forest, later with glimpses of Cefni saltmarsh. After a long straight section, turn RIGHT on the CP/HT along a side track, soon narrowing. At an open view to Malltraeth estuary, the CP/HT turn left along a narrow path at the open forest edge, then follow a wide sandy path through tall conifers, later descending and angling left.

2 At a track junction at post 14 the CP and Horse Trails split. Continue with the waymarked HT along the narrow track ahead. Later take the waymarked left fork through an area of small pines, then along the forest edge by sand dunes hiding Penrhos beach beyond to a waymarked red running trail post. (Here a path leads right over the dunes onto the beach offering a low tide walk along to Ynys Llanddwyn. Continue along the edge of Traeth Llanddwyn, then follow a blue waymarked trail up to point 3.) Continue along the now narrow path past the wood corner and on to a HT post embedded in the dunes, with a post stump nearby. (About 100 yards further is a wide gap in the dunes offering another beach option to Ynys Llanddwyn.)

Here follow a path leading left into the forest, then a narrow track to rejoin the CP on a wide stony track. Follow it RIGHT, soon bending inland.

3 At a waymarked CP/HT/blue walking trail turn RIGHT and follow the blue waymarked path down to meet a waymarked high tide path onto Traeth Llanddwyn, with Ynys Llanddwyn nearby. Return to point 3, then continue with the HT up the track, past where with the CP turns right, and on to post 8 where the Horse Trails split. Turn LEFT with the blue HT up a narrow green track. Later, when it angles left to a nearby stony track, keep ahead, over the track and follow a path opposite (a waymarked white trail in reverse) to a stony path by post 30. Follow it LEFT. Just before a kissing gate/gate at the forest edge bend LEFT along a wider stony path (a waymarked green cycle trail in reverse). At a track T-junction by post 31 turn RIGHT, now rejoined by the black HT. Shortly the track bends NW past partly hidden pools, then descends to picnic tables (with your outward track ahead). Here turn RIGHT along a path, over a footbridge, and on to join your outward track. Later at a board where the track bends towards the barrier/A4080 take a path on the left through trees. After bending left take its right fork. At a T-junction turn RIGHT, then at the next LEFT to reach the car park.

WALK 33

MALLTRAETH COB

DESCRIPTION A 2½ mile walk offering the opportunity to see red squirrels, reintroduced in 2004, on feeders by the forest car park before an enjoyable there and back walk following the Coastal Path along an early 19thC embankment, offering good views, various birdlife, a detailed information board and Thomas Telford's original tidal door. Malltraeth has a pub and café (*Wed-Sun 11-5*). Allow about 1½ hours. From Llyn Parc Mawr car park there is also an easy 1½ mile waymarked Red Squirrel Walk through the forest, featuring a view overlooking the hidden lake created in the 1980s as a habitat for birds.

START Llyn Parc Mawr car park [SH 414671] or car park in Malltraeth [SH 407688].

DIRECTIONS Llyn Parc Mawr car park lies on the eastern side of the A4080 1 mile south of Malltraeth. The car park in Malltraeth is opposite the side road

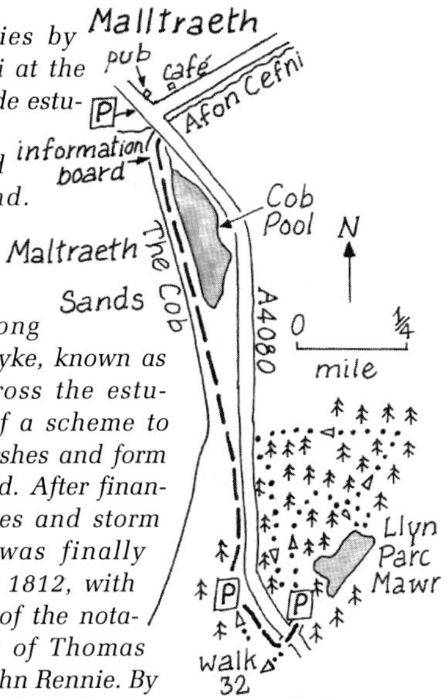

Malltraeth *lies by the Afon Ceni at the head of its wide estuary which used to extend further inland. In the late 18thC work began on building a long sea defence dyke, known as The Cob, across the estuary as part of a scheme to drain the marshes and form reclaimed land. After financial difficulties and storm breaches it was finally completed in 1812, with the oversight of the notable engineers of Thomas Telford and John Rennie. By 1824 the river had also been canalised. On The Cob's inland side is an attractive pool with the expansive Malltraeth Marsh beyond, which became an area of wet grassland meadows. On its seaward side is Malltraeth Bay. All these habitats support a rich variety of birdlife, reflected in the work of renowned wildlife illustrator Charles Tunnicliffe, who lived in Malltraeth from the late 1940's, on display at Oriel Ynys Mon, near Llangefni.*

1 Return to the A4080, cross to the forestry track opposite, then turn RIGHT and follow the waymarked Coastal Path alongside the forest to Pen Cob car park, then across The Cob to Malltraeth. After refreshments in the village simply retrace your steps enjoying the views and birdlife from a different perspective.

WALK 34
TRAETH MAWR

DESCRIPTION A 2¾ mile (**A**) or 2½ mile (**B**) walk featuring a tidal section of the Coastal Path (CP), a small river estuary, one of Anglesey's best beaches and an extensive area of dunes. Allow about 2 hours.
START Aberffraw car park [SH 357690].
DIRECTIONS The car park by the old bridge over the river, adjoins a minor road leading from the nearby A4080.

1 From the old packhorse bridge built in 1731 bend left with the road. Soon turn RIGHT past a barrier on the signposted Coastal Path towards the river Ffraw, then along the sand beside it, by the edge of dunes. Later continue along the fine sandy beach of Traeth Mawr below the large dunes. Near its end turn LEFT up through the dunes to follow a good path beside, or later a short distance from, a fence on the right across the impressive undulating landscape of Aberffraw Dunes, past side paths to a CP finger post onto the narrow road. (For **Walk B** follow it back to the start.)

2 Turn RIGHT then LEFT on a nearby signposted path. After a few yards take a path on the left. Follow it across the next area of dunes, with a fence to your right, then later at a cross-path follow it LEFT across the dunes towards Aberffraw and the start.

WALK 35
ST CWYFAN'S CHURCH

DESCRIPTION A 5½ mile (**A**) or 4¼ mile (**B**) featuring two ancient churches, notably St. Cwyfan's church situated on a tiny island. A shorter 2 mile walk (**C**) is included. After visiting Aberffraw's St Bueno's church an inland route is followed to Porth Cwyfan, from where St Cwyfan's church is accessible by a stone causeway at low tide (*check tide table*). It returns on the Coastal Path via Trwyn Du headland containing the remains of a Bronze Age burial cairn. Allow about 3 hours.
START Aberffraw car park [SH 357690].
DIRECTIONS See Walk 34.

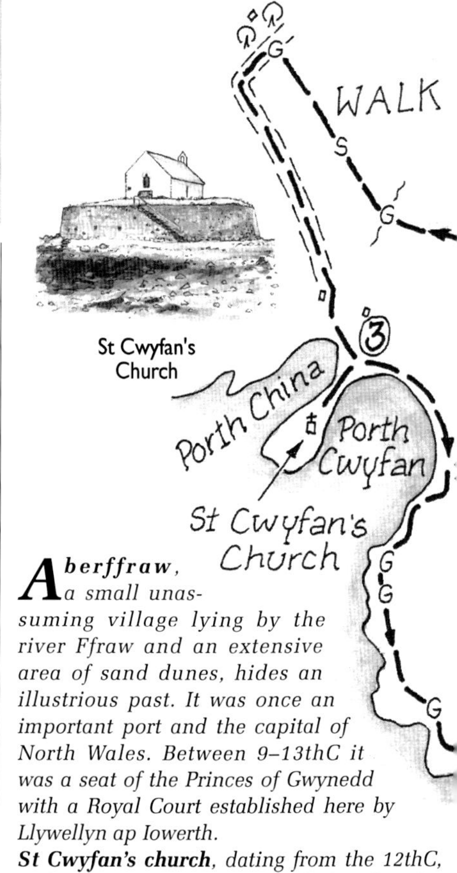

St Cwyfan's Church

Aberffraw, *a small unassuming village lying by the river Ffraw and an extensive area of sand dunes, hides an illustrious past. It was once an important port and the capital of North Wales. Between 9–13thC it was a seat of the Princes of Gwynedd with a Royal Court established here by Llywellyn ap Iowerth.*
St Cwyfan's church*, dating from the 12thC, with later additions, was founded in the 7thC and reputedly dedicated to an Irish saint. It was originally on the mainland but over time the sea eroded the boulder clay cliffs and massive stone walls were built to preserve the church. In 2008 an organ was presented to the church, which was carried across the causeway by the church warden and local farmers. I happened to be present when a specially made heavy wooden base for the organ was also carried across, and was privileged to provide photographs recording the event for inclusion in a time capsule beneath the organ. The sound of the organ being*

played in this ancient church was a delight.

1 Cross the old packhorse bridge built in 1731 and go up the road past The Crown pub. Beyond the junction bear LEFT with the road. At the next junction keep ahead to visit 12thC St Bueno's church. Turn LEFT past the nearby school, then RIGHT along Fronheulog to a kissing gate at its end. Follow the gated field path – *with good views along the estuary across to the Lleyn peninsula* – to the bend of a stony track which you follow past Penrhyn Gwyn cottages and a green track on the left. At a track T-junction, turn RIGHT. (Shortly, for **Walk C**, turn left along another hedge-lined green track, soon bending left down it, then follow an enclosed path down to join the Coastal Path at the foreshore.) Continue up the track to a road – *with a view of St Cwyfan's Church.* (For **Walk B** follow the road left down to Porth Cwyfan, then return along the Coastal Path.)

2 Turn RIGHT up the road past a picnic area at a great viewpoint, then a trig point – *enjoying extensive views from Snowdonia to Holyhead Mountain.* After ¼ mile, go through a kissing gate on the bend. Go up the field edge past an old kissing gate and down to another. Now go half-LEFT down the field to a gated footbridge in the corner. Go half-LEFT up the next field to a kissing gate. Continue ahead along the edge of the next large field to a kissing gate/gate. The path now heads half-right past the end of high ground to a stile/gate, then continues ahead across the next large field to a kissing gate onto a stony track. Follow it LEFT, later passing near Trac Mon motor racing circuit, then Tyn Twll to reach the foreshore at Porth China – *a name reflecting the extraction of boulder clay here.*

3 If your visit coincides with low tide you can visit nearby St Cwyfan's church. *Otherwise enjoy the view of this solitary island church surrounded by sea at high tide.* Follow the foreshore round Porth Cwyfan past the end of the road (Walk B) and a gate, then a path across rocks and go past a small sandy beach to a kissing gate. Now follow the delightful Coastal Path along the headland's low cliffs, with one short section of foreshore to eventually reach Trwyn Du. After diverting to its top containing a stone seat and embedded stones indicating the Bronze Age burial cairn, continue with the Coastal Path to another kissing gate, then along the shoreline near the river Ffraw, later with an alternative Coastal Path loop option, to a road leading to the old bridge.

WALK 36

BARCLODIAD Y GAWRES

DESCRIPTION A 4 mile walk from Rhosneigr featuring sections of the Coastal Path, beaches, sand dunes and a major Neolithic burial tomb. Allow about 2½ hours. The route can be shortened or varied by starting at other car parks shown or according to the tide, and extended to Llyn Maelor.

START Rhosneigr car park [SH 319730].

DIRECTIONS Turn off the main street past the Village Hall to the car park by the library.

*R**hosneigr**, now a peaceful seaside village, was once renowned for its inhabitants luring ships on to nearby rocks! Further south along the coast is Barclodiau y Gawres – a prominent grass mound containing Neolithic burial chambers with rare decorated large stones, dating from 2500–3000 BC. Nearby Porth Trecastell is better known as Cable Bay after it became the terminus of a telegraph cable link with Ireland in 1855. The link was extended to America in 1866 when a similar cable was laid across the Atlantic from Ireland, so establishing the first transatlantic communications service.*

1 Return to the main street and follow it LEFT – *later with a view across the bay to Rhoscolyn and Holyhead Mountain.* Follow the road round to Traeth Llydan (Broad Beach), where the signposted Coastal Path takes you onto the beach. Go along the beach past where at high tide the Coastal Path follows the river into the dunes. Later, just before houses, go up through the dunes past a large telegraph pole to a path junction. Bear RIGHT on the waymarked Coastal Path to a lane just behind the houses. Follow the Coastal Path through dunes and over a nearby road to a kissing gate. Continue on the Coastal Path behind the dunes to reach a car park with toilets and information panel at Porth Tyn Tywyn. Keep ahead and follow the signposted Coastal Path through the dunes just above the beach, later passing close by a cottage.

2 At a waymarked path junction, the Coastal Path bears RIGHT and continues along the headland, then rises to Barclodiau y Gawres. After peering inside its gated entrance retrace your steps. Just before the waymarked path junction gain access to the beach at Porth Nobla. Walk along the beach towards Traeth Llydan, later near the sand dunes. Just before the houses passed earlier turn RIGHT up through the dunes to join your outward route at the access road. Follow the waymarked Coastal Path through the extensive dunes past the nearby Oystercatcher café, bar and restaurant, which you may be tempted to visit, to eventually cross a footbridge over the river. Turn RIGHT and follow the riverside path to a small car park by the A4080. Follow the main road into Rhosneigr.

WALK 37

LLYN MAELOG

DESCRIPTION A 2¼ mile walk of contrasting coastal and inland scenery at Rhosneigr. After a choice of Coastal Path routes through the dunes (**a**) or along the beach (**b**) the walk continues inland to Llyn Maelor, then follows a waymarked around the attractive lake. Allow about 1½ hours.

START A4080 car park [SH 321727].

DIRECTIONS The small car park is on the eastern outskirts of the village near a road bridge on the A4080.

*L**lyn Maelor** is a small shallow nutrient rich lake, a designated Site of Special Scientific Interest, that provides a habitat for a variety of birds, including wintering wildfowl. It takes its name from a 6thC Saint. In the late 18thC small ships were built on its shore. Until 1968 it was the water supply for the village. It is a popular fishing lake and in 2011 became the first lake in Wales to be classified as a village green.*

1 Just before the nearby bridge follow a path leading right, taking its left fork through bulrushes, then by the river to a footbridge over it. (For **route b** continue ahead to Traeth

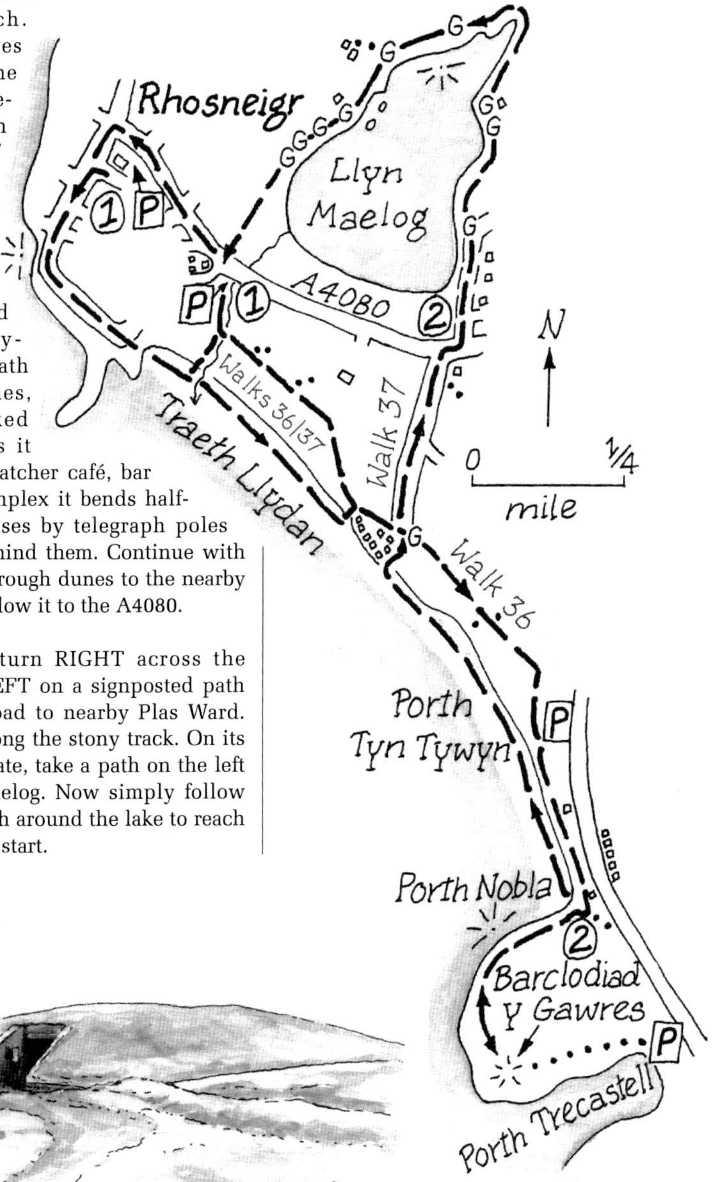

Llydan and walk along the beach. Just before houses go up through the dunes past a telegraph pole to join the Coastal Path/ route a to reach their access road. Follow it to point 2.) For **route a** cross the footbridge and follow the waymarked Coastal Path through the dunes, past a waymarked path junction. As it nears The Oystercatcher café, bar and restaurant complex it bends half-right towards houses by telegraph poles to reach a lane behind them. Continue with the Coastal Path through dunes to the nearby access road and follow it to the A4080.

2 Cross it and turn RIGHT across the bridge, then LEFT on a signposted path along an access road to nearby Plas Ward. Continue ahead along the stony track. On its bend at a kissing gate, take a path on the left to nearby Llyn Maelog. Now simply follow the waymarked path around the lake to reach the A4080 near the start.

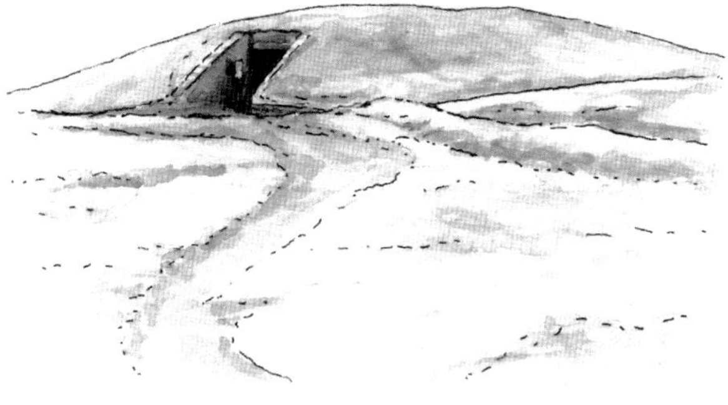

Rhosneigr
Llyn Maelog
A4080
Walk 37
Walks 36/37
Walk 36
Traeth Llydan
Porth Tyn Tywyn
Porth Nobla
Barclodiad y Gawres
Porth Trecastell
N
0
1/4
mile

Barclodiad y Gawres

WALK 38

TRAETH LLYDAN

DESCRIPTION A 3¾ mile walk follows field paths and a minor road down to Borthwen, with its fine sandy beach. It then follows the Coastal Path (CP) east along low cliffs to Traeth Llydan's sandy beach and inland, before returning past The White Eagle pub. Allow about 2½ hours.

START St Gwenfaen's church, Rhoscolyn [SH 268757] or car park with toilets Borthwen [SH 272 752].

DIRECTIONS From the B4545 between Treaddur and Four Mile Bridge two minor roads lead 2 miles to Rhoscolyn, where there is parking near the church, (except Sunday mornings) or continue past The White Eagle to the beach car park and return along the road to point 2.

A **church** *has stood on this site since 630 AD when St. Gwenfaen established her cell here. The present church dates from the 1870s using stones from an earlier 15thC church.*

1 Follow the minor road past the church, then at the churchyard corner take the signposted path through a small gate. Follow it beside the wall to a stone stile and kissing gate. Go across an access track to a ladder-stile. Follow the path through two fields and kissing gates to an access track, through a small gate opposite and on to another by Ty Werl. Follow the waymarked path past the house to the bend of a road. Go down the road.

2 On the bend by Glan Towyn take the signposted enclosed Coastal Path past Borthwen beach. At a waymarked path junction go through a nearby hidden blue gate ahead and follow the path to Cilbwch. Go along its access track, then at a junction, follow the track RIGHT past Borth Esgob to a kissing gate. Follow the well waymarked CP across the headland, then along the low cliffs round to Porth Cae-du and a kissing gate. After sleeper bridges go across a field to another kissing gate. Continue with the CP – *with views across to Rhosneigr and RAF Valley* – later passing a flagpole above Traeth Llydan. Follow the CP down onto the sandy beach and along its edge.

3 After 200 yards at a life-buoy, take the stepped CP up the dunes and through the pine forest to a kissing gate. After another the CP heads to Bryn-y-bar. Continue along its access track, then attractive road past a wood, then a CP route. At a junction turn RIGHT past Ty Lon, then go through a kissing gate on the left by an access track. Follow the kissing gated path to cottages at Rhoscolyn, then their access track to the bend of the road. (If starting at Borthyn you can shorten the walk by following the road ahead.) Follow the road RIGHT past The White Eagle pub. At the next junction turn LEFT to St Gwenfaen's church.

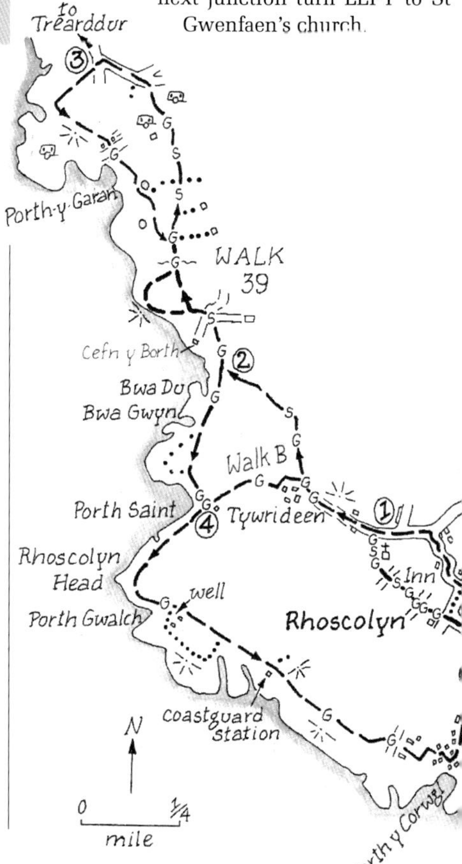

WALK 39
BWA DU

DESCRIPTION A 5 mile (**A**), 3½ mile (**B**) or 3¼ mile (**C**) walk exploring a section of the Coastal Path (CP), featuring the splendid sea arches of Bwa Du and Bwa Gwyn, and impressive ancient St Gwenfaen's Well. Allow about 3 hours. From Borthwen start at point 5.
START As Walk 38.

1 From the church follow the road west to Lodge Bach, then continue along a track. Just before Tywrideen go through a kissing gate on the right and down to a small gate. Go down the middle of the long field to a kissing gate and a ladder-stile ahead. Just beyond follow a path LEFT through gorse then bracken, soon heading towards the large white shoreline house of Cefn y Borth down to the Coastal Path. (For **Walk C** follow it left to point 4.)

2 Follow it RIGHT up to a kissing gate and on to a stone stile/gate at the entrance to Cefn y Borth. Just beyond turn LEFT beside the wall, then at a CP waymark post turn RIGHT, soon descending and continuing to a kissing gate. Go past a small sandy cove to another kissing gate. Turn LEFT then immediately angle RIGHT on another waymarked path to pass through a gateway. Just beyond bear RIGHT with the path, soon taking its waymarked left fork, past a stone stile, over a cross-path and up a small gully to another stone stile. Follow the path to a kissing gate just before a caravan site. Follow the enclosed path up to an access road. Follow it LEFT to a road junction. Turn LEFT on the signposted CP briefly along The Lee Caravan Park's driveway.

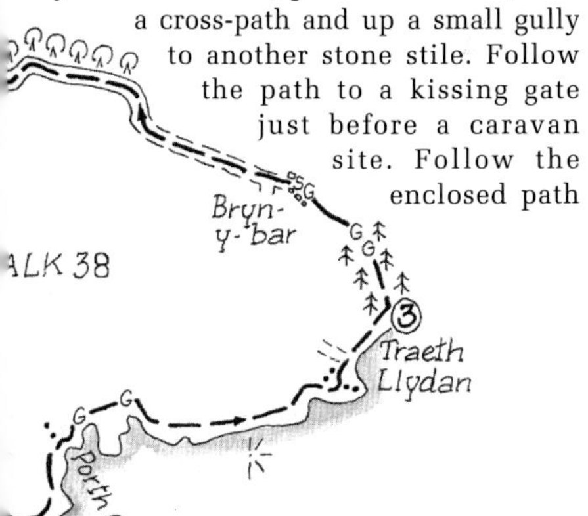

3 Turn RIGHT and follow the CP to low cliffs. After passing above the caravan site the CP descends between static caravans to the site's access road and a kissing gate above Porth-y-garan. Follow the CP past a reedy pool, a private gate and on beside an old wall, at its corner bending left to join your outward route. After the second kissing gate follow the CP round the small headland to rejoin your outward route near Cefn y Borth. Follow it back to point 2 then continue on the CP past Bwa Du and Bwa Gwyn then above Porth Saint. (For **Walk B** just after a kissing gate turn left through another. Follow the waymarked path inland, up to Tywrideen and round its boundary wall to join your outward route.)

4 After crossing a footbridge continue with the CP near the large wall across Rhoscolyn Head and round above Porth Gwalch to a kissing gate. The CP passes medieval St Gwenfaen's Well – *said to cure mental disorders by throwing white quartz pebbles into the water* – continues to Rhoscolyn Coastguard Station, then descends – *with a view of nearby Rhoscolyn Beacon on a tiny island* – to a kissing gate. Soon after passing a wall corner angle left to a kissing gate in the boundary corner. Follow the enclosed CP, shortly passing dwellings, and descending to a stony track by Boatmen's Cottage above Porth y Corwgl. Continue along the track down to the shore and along the edge of Borthwen Bay. After the last white cottage take a raised path above the beach to the car park.

5 Go along the road, then later on a bend by The Point go into Ty Werl's entrance ahead. Follow a waymarked enclosed path to a small gate and on to another by a track. Go through a kissing gate opposite and through two fields up to a ladder-stile. Go half-LEFT across an access track to a kissing gate and stone stile at the churchyard corner and on to the road leading to the start.

WALK 40

PORTH DAFARCH

DESCRIPTION A 10½ mile exploration of the western coast and hinterland of Holy Island, now linked to Anglesey by two bridges. The coastline consists of some of the oldest pre-Cambrian rocks in Britain. After visiting nearby historic roundhouses the route follows the Coastal Path (CP) along the cliffs to Porth Dafarch, then takes a meandering route inland via two Open Access areas to Holyhead Mountain. It then heads west to Ellin's Tower and refreshments at the Visitor Centre café. Allow about 6 hours. An enjoyable 1 mile walk linking the Visitor Centre, Ellin's Tower and the hut circles can easily be made.

START RSPB Ellin's Tower car park [SH 211819] or RSPB Visitor Centre car park. [SH 208821].

DIRECTIONS The car park adjoins a minor road leading to South Stack accessed from Holyhead or Treaddur Bay. The Visitor Centre is further along. (From the Centre take a stepped path down to Ellin's Tower then follow a choice of paths to the Tower's car park.)

1 After visiting the nearby historic site containing about 50 buildings dating from the Iron Age to Post Roman times go down the road to a junction and take the signposted Coastal Path through a small gate. The path runs parallel with the road, then crosses it to a kissing gate. Go across the field to the far boundary overlooking the sea. Now follow the waymarked CP to a rocky headland, along the cliffs above Porth y Gwin, round the next headland, above the inlet at Porth Ruffydd, then along the cliffs to eventually reach the sandy beach of Porth Dafarch.

2 From the toilets, follow the CP across the National Trust headland and along the cliff tops then inland to follow an access track up to the road. Follow it RIGHT. After Moryn. in a dip, take a signposted path along Isallt Fawr's access track. Keep with the right fork to the last large house, then follow a path through trees to a kissing gate. Go along the long field edge to a stile/gate and an enclosed path to a kissing gate onto a stony track. Follow it RIGHT past dwellings. Later at a road turn LEFT, then take a signposted enclosed path on the right to a stile and go across a long meadow to a kissing gate by houses to a road beyond. Turn LEFT, then at the T-junction LEFT again along the pavement opposite.

South Stack

lighthous

Ellin's Towe

3 Shortly, take a signposted path over a ladder-stile. Follow the enclosed path up and round to a stile. Go half-LEFT to a waymark post and across the field to a ladder-stile into Mynydd-celyn-mawr, an Open Access area. Follow the path ahead through gorse to a wide clearing. Angle LEFT towards distinct rocks on the low gorse ridge, and follow a path rising across them, then up over another rock to a waymark post. Turn RIGHT a few yards, then LEFT up across rock slabs to a boulder, by another in gorse. Keep ahead across the open scrubland towards Holyhead Mountain, with a bungalow half-left. Soon head half-RIGHT down the rough pasture, grazed by wild ponies, to a waymarked old gate in the corner and a nearby small gate. Turn LEFT up the road.

4 At the top go through a kissing gate on the right and another ahead hidden by gorse. Go half-LEFT to a waymark post and round to a kissing gate. Follow the path across an Open Access area of gorse, heather and scrub, later passing an old gatepost. Just before a kissing gate, follow the path LEFT to another. Continue ahead, soon beside a wall, to Cae-alltwen. The delightful path continues by a fence, then bends left, passing beneath small crags, to eventually reach a kissing gate. Follow the path ahead through bracken/gorse, shortly bending and continuing with the boundary to a half ladder-stile. Angle RIGHT and follow the waymarked path through a boundary and small field to a kissing gate, then across a small field. When it splits keep ahead through gorse, bending right to a waymark post, then left to a kissing gate. The path now angles LEFT across the

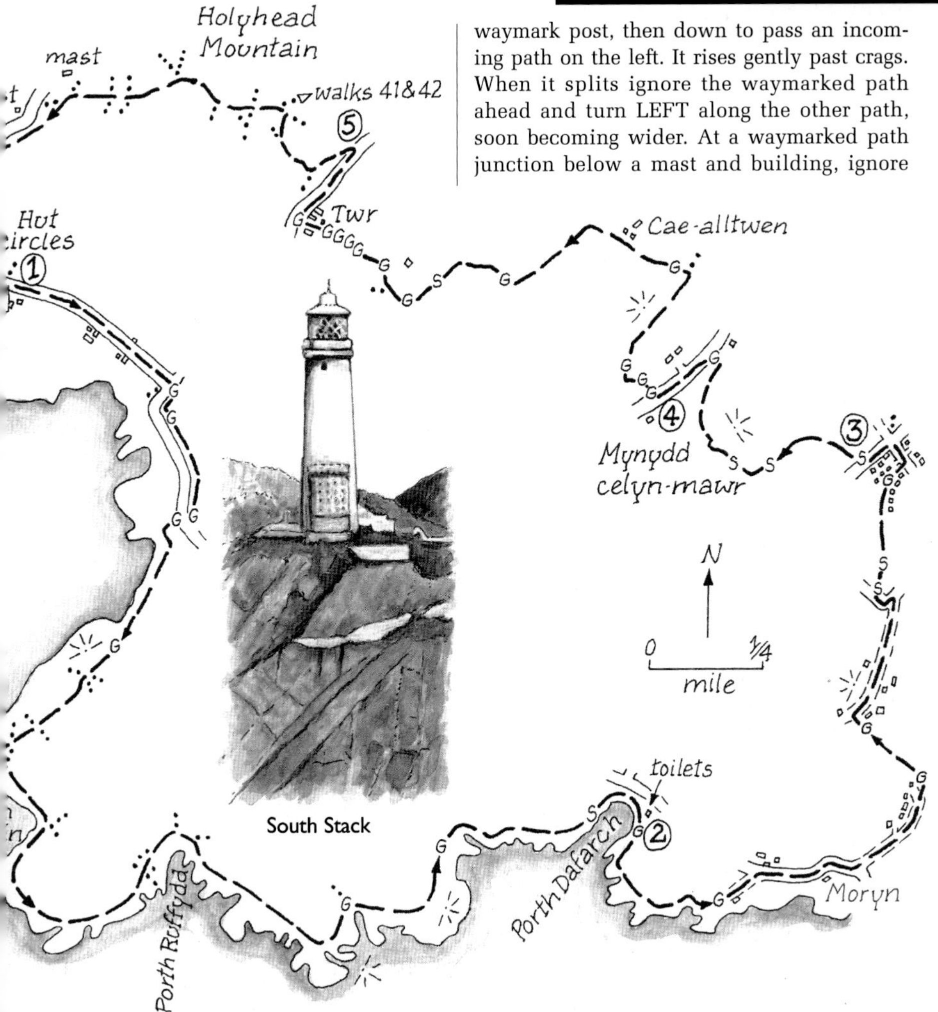

South Stack

field to a waymark post and down to a gateway. Go along the edge of two fields through gates, and on to a hidden small gate. Pass through gates at Twr farm onto a road. Follow it RIGHT.

5 Shortly, take a signposted path angling back up a stony track. Immediately after it bends right take a stony path on the left up through heather and gorse. It levels out, briefly accompanies a wall, then crosses it. Take its right fork to a waymark post, then bend left up to another at a cross-path beneath Holyhead Mountain. Follow it LEFT. Soon, when it splits, take the stony right fork past a waymark post, then down to pass an incoming path on the left. It rises gently past crags. When it splits ignore the waymarked path ahead and turn LEFT along the other path, soon becoming wider. At a waymarked path junction below a mast and building, ignore the waymarked Coastal Path, and turn immediately LEFT along a rough stony path. It soon passes close to an access road for the other transmitter mast nearby, then joins it. Go down the road then take a stony path on the left, opposite a nearby large reedy lake, along a small ridge and down to a car park. Take the signposted CP down to Ellin's Tower – *built in 1868 and now an RSPB Centre, offering good views of South Stack lighthouse.* For refreshments (or returning to the alternative start) take a stone stepped path up to the Visitor Centre café, then return to follow either a wide stony path or the clifftop CP back to Ellin's Tower car park.

WALK 41

NORTH & SOUTH STACKS

DESCRIPTION An exhilarating anti-clockwise undulating 5¼ mile walk around rocky Holyhead Mountain, with its high cliffs and extensive views. The route follows the Coastal Path (CP) to the former Fog Signal Station at North Stack then passes an optional short climb to the mountain's summit (721 feet/220 metres), The CP continues to the headland overlooking South Stack lighthouse – open to visitors (*check times*) – and descends to RSPB's 19thC Ellin's Tower for views of the bird-nesting cliffs. After refreshments at the Visitor Centre cafe it returns by other waymarked paths. Allow about 3½ hours. The paths are good, but this is real mountain terrain and best avoided in poor visibility.

START Holyhead Breakwater Country Park Visitor Centre [SH 226833].

DIRECTIONS The Country Park lies beneath Holyhead Mountain and is signposted from the northern end of Holyhead.

In the 19th century *navigational aids were needed to help protect the coastal shipping and assist ships travelling between Ireland and Holyhead. In 1809 Trinity House, at a cost of £12,000, established a lighthouse on South Stack, a small rocky island connected to the mainland by a small bridge. In 1938 its oil lamps were replaced by electric powered lamps, then in 1987 its light became fully automated. A Fog Signal Station was also built on the cliffs by North Stack. Its ornate Magazine stored gunpowder for a cannon that was fired to warn ships away from the cliffs in fog. Late 19thC it was replaced by an oil-fired siren.*

1 From the Centre go through the car park to a wall gap, then follow a path past nearby Llyn Llwynog to a stony track. Follow it LEFT, soon joined by the Coastal Path, which you follow through a kissing gate on the right. Later the CP crosses the steep slopes above the sea, then rises past a small stone building – *once used by the quarry to store explosives* – increasingly more steeply, to a cross-path. Follow it RIGHT, soon rising, then take the right fork down to the former Fog Signal Station. Go up a zig-zagging stony track. At a crossroad of tracks/paths, turn RIGHT, then take the left fork up to a good viewpoint towards South Stack. The CP then descends – *with the summit trig point visible ahead* – passes through heather and goes up the right fork.

2 On a small rise at a waymark post you can make a short steep climb to the summit, returning via another path signed to South Stack, passing the ramparts of the Iron Age hillfort. The CP now descends past side paths to a waymarked path junction below a building and transmitter mast, then crosses a road. It passes another mast and continues past reedy pools to a lookout shelter overlooking South Stack lighthouse, then descends to the road, where 400 steps lead down to South Stack. Follow the road past another (your return route) and at a car park follow the CP down to Ellin's Tower. Now take a stone stepped path up to the Visitor Centre, then follow the road back up to join your return route. Later, when the narrow road bends towards the mast, follow a wide stony path to the right of it to a familiar crossroad of paths. Turn RIGHT and follow the waymarked path past side paths, later bending right beneath Holyhead Mountain, then rising across its shoulder, past side paths and continuing near a wall on your left.

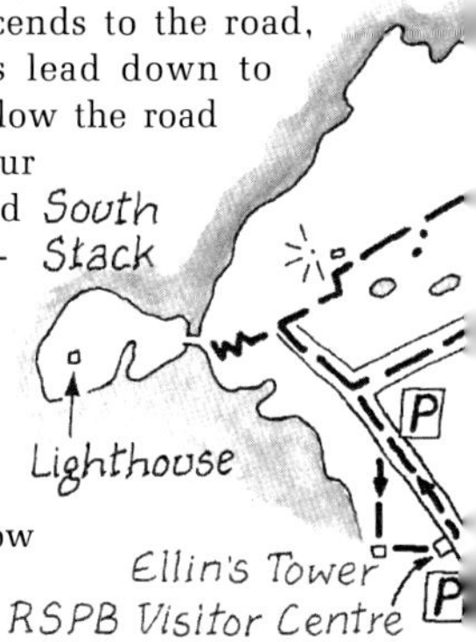

3 At the wall corner keep ahead. Later at path crossroads continue ahead with the waymarked walled path. At the wall corner the path descends – *with a good view overlooking Holyhead breakwater* – to a lane, then turns left to a road. Follow it LEFT to its end by Gornish. Take the signposted path past the house ahead and down the hillside,

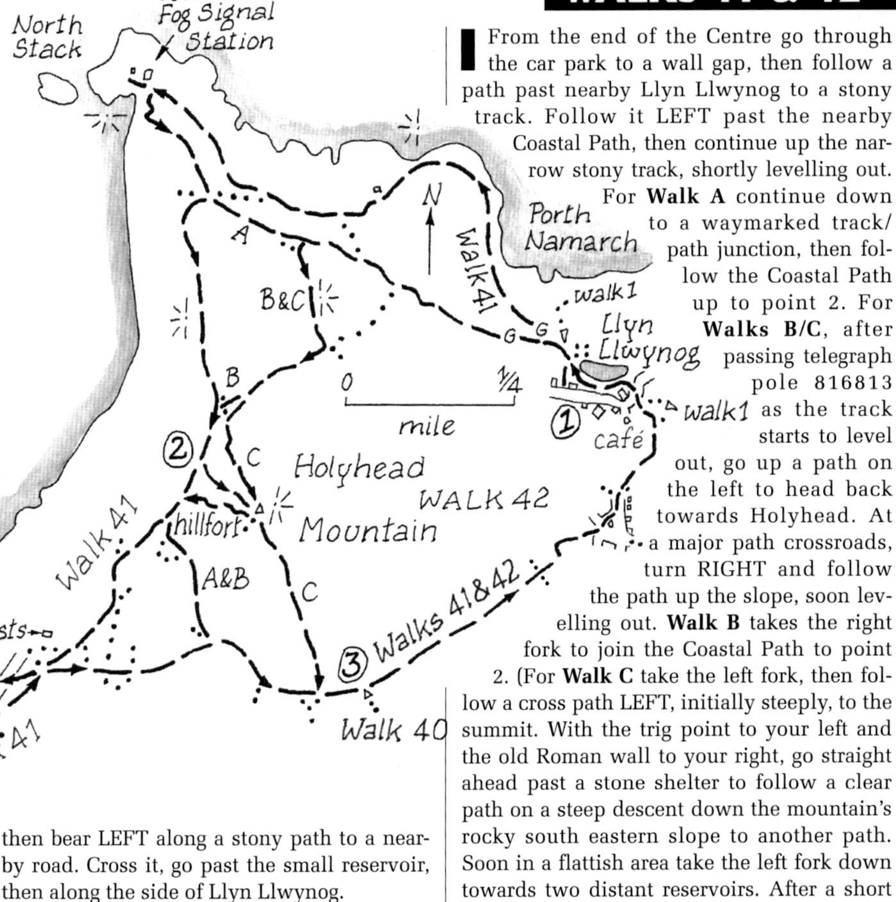

then bear LEFT along a stony path to a nearby road. Cross it, go past the small reservoir, then along the side of Llyn Llwynog.

WALK 42

HOLYHEAD MOUNTAIN

DESCRIPTION A choice of 2¾ mile (**A**), 2¼ mile (**B**) or 2½ mile (**C**) meandering walks to the summit of Holyhead Mountain (721 feet/ 220 metres), with its remains of a Roman watch-tower and Iron Age hillfort. Walks A & B take the signed ascent/descent from the Coastal Path. Walk C has a more demanding rocky descent. Allow about 2 hours. Despite its low height this is real mountain terrain and should be avoided in poor visibility.

START As Walk 41.

1 From the end of the Centre go through the car park to a wall gap, then follow a path past nearby Llyn Llwynog to a stony track. Follow it LEFT past the nearby Coastal Path, then continue up the narrow stony track, shortly levelling out. For **Walk A** continue down to a waymarked track/ path junction, then follow the Coastal Path up to point 2. For **Walks B/C**, after passing telegraph pole 816813 as the track starts to level out, go up a path on the left to head back towards Holyhead. At a major path crossroads, turn RIGHT and follow the path up the slope, soon levelling out. **Walk B** takes the right fork to join the Coastal Path to point 2. (For **Walk C** take the left fork, then follow a cross path LEFT, initially steeply, to the summit. With the trig point to your left and the old Roman wall to your right, go straight ahead past a stone shelter to follow a clear path on a steep descent down the mountain's rocky south eastern slope to another path. Soon in a flattish area take the left fork down towards two distant reservoirs. After a short steep descent a more level path takes you to a wall gap. Beyond at a crossroad of paths, turn LEFT and follow instructions in paragraph 3 of Walk 39.)

2 At the top of the rise, take the signed short steep climb to the summit, returning via another path signed to South Stack, passing the ramparts of an Iron Age hillfort. Follow the Coastal Path LEFT, then turn LEFT along a waymarked path beneath the mountain's rocky western slopes, popular with rock climbers, soon descending to a path junction. Turn LEFT along the waymarked path, soon rising across the mountain's shoulder and continuing near a wall on your left. Now follow instructions in paragraph 3 of Walk 41.

PRONUNCIATION

Welsh	*English equivalent*
c	always hard, as in cat
ch	as in the Scottish word loch
dd	as th in then
f	as f in **of**
ff	as ff in **off**
g	always hard as in got
ll	no real equivalent. It is like 'th' in then, but with an 'L' sound added to it, giving 'thlan' for the pronunciation of the Welsh 'Llan'.

In Welsh the accent usually falls on the last-but-one syllable of a word.

KEY TO THE MAPS

- Walk route and direction
- Metalled road
- Unsurfaced road
- Footpath/route adjoining walk route
- River/stream
- Trees
- Railway
- G Gate
- S Stile
- F.B. Footbridge
- Viewpoint
- P Parking
- T Telephone

Useful information
Isle of Anglesey County Council:
Rights of Way Section 01248 752367
Coastal Path 01248 752381
Email: pemht@anglesey.gov.uk for both

Published by **Kittiwake-Books Limited**
3 Glantwymyn Village Workshops, Glantwymyn, Machynlleth, Montgomeryshire SY20 8LY

Drawings by Morag Perrott
Cover photos: Main: West coast (Walk 3)
Inset: 'White Ladies' (Walks 4 & 5). David Berry

Printed by Mixam, UK.

ISBN: **978 1 908748 45 4**

THE COUNTRYSIDE CODE

- Be safe – plan ahead and follow any signs
- Leave gates and property as you find them
- Protect plants and animals, and take your litter home
- Keep dogs under close control
- Consider other people

Open Access
Whilst most routes follow public rights of way or established permissive paths, some cross areas of land where walkers have the legal right of access under The CRoW Act 2000. Open Access land is detailed on OS Explorer 262 and 263 maps covering Anglesey. Access can be subject to restrictions and closure for land management or safety reasons for up to 28 days a year. Please respect any notices.

About the author, David Berry

David is an experienced walker with a love of the countryside and an interest in local history. He is the author of a series of walks guidebooks covering North Wales, where he has lived and worked for many years. He has written for Walking Wales and Ramblers Walk magazines. He has also worked as a Rights of Way surveyor across North Wales and served as a member of Denbighshire Local Access Forum.

Whether on a riverside ramble, mountain or long distance walk, he greatly appreciates the beauty, culture and history of the landscape and hopes that his comprehensive guidebooks will encourage people to explore on foot its diverse scenery and rich heritage. For more information visit www.davidberrywalks.co.uk